SIX-MINUTE X-R

SIX-MINUTE X-RAY

RAPID BEHAVIOR PROFILING

CHASE HUGHES

We rise by lifting others.

ISBN: 978-1-7351416-0-2

Evergreen Press
November, 2020
Milton, Delaware

Interior Formatting: Rachael Ritchey

*Dedicated to the ghost soldier of the
Yorktown Victory Monument.*

TABLE OF CONTENTS

Epigraph .... **xiii**

Introduction... **xv**

ONE: Skills & Techniques **1**

Mastery 2

Surgeon - Level 4..2

Nurse - Level 3 3

Paramedic - Level 2..3

Grey's Anatomy Guy - Level 1 4

Knowledge Vs. Skill 4

"The 2/3 Rule"..6

The Human Brain..7

You're Competing with Social Media........................10

The 'Wait till the End' Fallacy 11

The Word 'Decision'...12

Summary 13

TWO: Seeing People in a New Way **14**

Law 1: Everyone is Suffering and Insecure...............15

Law 2: Everyone is Wearing a Mask 16

Law 3: Everyone is Pretending Not to Wear a Mask........17

Law 4: Everyone is a Product of Childhood Suffering and Reward 17

The Four Lenses to Seeing People 19

People are Broken 20

People are Different..20

People are Facts 21

People are Reasons 21

Summary 22

THREE: Behavior Skills **23**

The Behavioral Table of Elements 25

The Cell Key 27

Architecture 28

Colors 29

Deception 30

Summary 30

    Knowledge Check 31

FOUR: The Eyes **32**

Blink Rate...33

Gestural Hemispheric Tendency (Ght) 38

Eye Home 41

    Shutter Speed..44

    Pupil Dilation 46

    Confirmation Glances..48

    The Eyebrow Flash..49

    Summary 51

FIVE: The Face **52**

Lip Compression...53

Object Insertion 54

True Vs. False Facial Expressions....................................55

The Stop Vs. Fade of Expressions 56

The Asymmetry of False Expressions 57

    The Artificial Smile 57

    Nostril Flaring 58

    Hushing...59

    Summary 61

    Knowledge Check 61

SIX: The Body **62**

Crossed Arms 62

Genital Protection...64

The Fig Leaf 64

The Single-Arm Wrap 65

Digital Extention 67

Digital Flexion 68

Fidgeting...70

Feet Honesty...70

Arms Behind Back 71

Handedness..72

Breathing Location 74

Shoulder Movement 76

    The Shoulder Shrug.......................................76

    The Single-Sided Shrug 77

Barrier Behavior 78

Hand to Chest...79

Hygienic Behavior..80

Summary 81

SEVEN: Deception Detection and Stress 82

    About Lying 83

        Hesitancy..84

        Psychological Distancing 85

        Rising Pitch 86

        Increased Speed 87

        Non-Answers...88

        Pronoun Absence.....................................88

        Resume Statements 89

        Non-Contractions 90

        Question Reversal 92

        Ambiguity...92

        Politeness...93

        Over Apologies 93

        Mini- Confessions 94

        Exclusions..96

        Chronology 97

        Confirmation Glance...............................98

        Pre-Swallow Movement 99

        Single-Sided Shrug................................100

        Throat Clasping......................................100

        Hushing..101

The Fig Leaf 102
Single-Arm Wrap..103
Elbow-Closure 104
Downward Palms 104
Summary 106
EIGHT: Elicitation **107**
How Elicitation Works...108
Elicitation Skills: Part One..110
The Hourglass Method 110
The Human Factors that Make Elicitation Possible ..112
The Need to Be Recognized...112
Diffidence 112
Correcting the Record...113
We Want to Be Heard 113
We Want to Offer Advice 113
We Will Offer Information to Those that Disagree...113
Elicitation Skills: Part Two..114
For Conversations 114
Provocative Statements 114
Informational Altruism..116
Flattery...118
Eliciting Complaints 119
Citations 121
Verbal Reflection 123
Naïveté 126
Criticism 128
Bracketing...129
Disbelief..131
Summary 132
Knowledge Check 133
NINE: The Human Needs Map...**134**
The Primary Social Needs 136
Significance...137
Approval / Recognition 138
Acceptance 140

Secondary Social Needs......................................141
    Intelligence..141
    Pity..142
    Strength/ Power......................................144
Identifying Human Needs in Conversation.....................145
Revealing Hidden Fears.....................................148
What the Needs Actually Mean - The Scary Part...........151
    Neuropeptides..151
Summary..155
    Locus of Control......................................156
    Knowledge Check....................................159
TEN: The Decision Map©..160
The Decision Map Unpacked....................................161
Buying a Cell Phone Case..165
Summary..169
ELEVEN: Sensory Preference Identification..............170
Summary..178
TWELVE: Pronoun Identification..........................179
Self Pronouns..180
Team Pronouns...180
Others Pronouns...181
    Knowledge Checkpoint.............................182
Summary..183
THIRTEEN: The Use of Adjectives..........................184
Summary..188
FOURTEEN: How Compliance Works.........................189
FIFTEEN: The Quadrant..193
How the Quadrant Makes Your Training Easy..............197
    Using the Quadrant in Conversations.........198
    Quadrant Elements.................................199
SIXTEEN: The Behavior Compass............................204
Summary..209

SEVENTEEN: How it Works for Influence: Critical Scenarios 210

    Scenario 1: Clinician (Emily) 211
    Scenario 2: Sales (David) 215

EIGHTEEN: Your Training Plan 220

    The Visual Phase 221
    The Audio Phase...223
    The Response Phase 224
    The Mental Phase 226
    The Training Plan..226

Final Thoughts 239

About the Author 240

Acknowledgments 241

Desiderata 243

Also by Chase Hughes.......................................245

Want the Full Cia-Level Training? 247

EPIGRAPH

There are countless things hidden behind the masks that people wear:

- Insecurity
- Fear
- Disagreement
- Shame
- Anger
- Resistance
- Objection
- Social needs
- Secret decisions
- Admiration
- Envy
- Emotional triggers
- Hidden desires and drives
- Shrouded intent
- Motivation-driving beliefs

I'm about to show you how to reveal all of them in less than six minutes. You bought this book for a reason: to get results. Let's get started

INTRODUCTION

People were dying. I wanted to stop it.

I dropped my pen onto the fresh, new legal pad in front of me after a four-day body language course. I hadn't written a single note. After ten years of research and training, I had discovered something awful.

Amidst an endless sea of 'experts,' no one had put together a system to read human behavior in a way that reveals explicitly what's hidden beneath.

The book you're holding is the missing piece that I spent twenty years in search of. After a year in the US Navy, I became increasingly obsessed with human behavior.

The body language training I took didn't work, and the books I read, with promising titles like 'Read Anyone Anytime,' never delivered. After a decade of research and development, I created the system you now hold in your hands.

I designed the Six-Minute X-ray system to be the most dangerous people-reading system in the world.

Relying on simple, outdated behavior analysis methods was not good enough for our critical intelligence operations, and it's clearly not good enough for you; someone who wants an edge.

There's one phrase you'll hear in every elite military training school:

"Never find yourself in a fair fight."

This means that if you're engaged with an opponent, the balance of power should be massively asymmetrical. Your skills, training, equipment, planning, and prowess should far exceed your opponent's.

While our military took this advice when it came to combat training, I discovered that the same principles didn't apply to intelligence recruiting, interrogation, psychological operations, and human intelligence collection. That is why I built the 6MX.

If you're reading this, you've probably already discovered a few things:

1. Most body language training is interesting but doesn't give you the edge you thought it would
2. A one-size-fits-all approach won't cut it when the stakes are high
3. There's a lot more to human behavior than most people know
4. Books on how to 'read people' don't deliver on that promise

After two decades of research, experimentation, and in-field work, I've developed the 6MX, the cornerstone of the Behavior Pilot system that lays the groundwork to see behind the mask, connect on a completely different level, and see the entire world in a way no one else can.

The skills you're about to learn will change your life. Less than 1% of people have them, but many *think* they do.

At Applied Behavior Research, training is designed for the **one-match-left** scenario: where there's no second chance and no opportunity to explain away failure.

My editor convinced me to add this line to the book, but I was hesitant. In my military training, I tell all my students one thing:

> *If you get kidnapped and stripped of your belongings, I want you to **still** have these skills. They should be in your head, not in a book. Take the superpowers you're about to learn and bring them to life. Nothing you're about to learn belongs locked in a notebook somewhere — these skills are designed to reside <u>in your head</u>.*

Keep in touch!
I can be reached any time at
www.chasehughes.com

I would sincerely love to hear how you're implementing these incredible skills in your life.

SIX-MINUTE X-RAY

CHAPTER 1

SKILLS & TECHNIQUES

We can trace almost all of our failures back to three things:

1. Our Communication
2. Our Observation
3. Our Behavior

Communication:

When we communicate, we persuade. We do it all the time, whether we're convincing someone to try a new restaurant or interviewing for a job. We can trace many of our failures back to communication and how we failed to persuade someone, or a group of people, into adopting our way of thinking.

Observation:

We can all look back and find several events that we regret. In many of them, we overlooked red flags, or we didn't recognize red flags or behavioral clues that we should have. Observation entails not only reading people, but situations.

How well we can observe the world drastically changes how we interact with it. Lack of observation, and inability to see the truth, have been responsible for many issues in our past.

Behavior:
How we manage and carry ourselves matters a lot. Something as simple as a poor choice of habits has resulted in failure for us before. The way we speak, walk, talk, move, and interact with people tells them a lot about us. Sometimes, even with our best intentions, we fail to get the outcome we want, not knowing the whole time that someone might have a 'gut feeling' about us that sets the stage for failure from the beginning.

MASTERY

Mastery over a topic is easy to gain, if you put in the work. In my (extremely basic) estimation, there are four levels of mastery.

SURGEON - LEVEL 4

At the top level, we have a person who's put in countless hours toward a specific skill. It's not the classroom education that gave them this level of expertise. It's the ingrained *skills* they have spent years honing. Although education is necessary, no one's a surgeon without thousands of hours of practice and repetition. We would never allow someone to cut us open and mess with our organs if they hadn't done it before. We want the experience, the reputation, that comes from thousands of hours of practice.

I'd like you to get to this level, and I think you'll be amazed when you discover just how fast you can do it. It may have taken me twenty-two years to develop the 6MX system, but I've done it in a way that makes it easy to learn and even easier to adapt into a skill.

The skill part is on you, however. I'm the college that educated you and gave you the degree. The practice is up to you. I wish I could be there right now with you to walk you through the steps, but I have faith that once you see how powerful this is, you'll be as addicted as I was. My job is to show you how powerful this is and get you juuuuust addicted enough to keep going in daily practice and become a behavioral surgeon.

NURSE - LEVEL 3

The nurse has put in the hours of practice but can still never accomplish what the surgeon is capable of. The nurse has put in the work for the education and is able to perform some complex tasks and diagnoses with the skills.

The nurse knows a lot about medicine and still knows enough to be dangerous, but doesn't see the world as a surgeon.

PARAMEDIC - LEVEL 2

The paramedic went through an education that allows them to use a variety of limited skills. It's easier to get to this level and doesn't take that long relative to the others.

GREY'S ANATOMY GUY - LEVEL 1

In level one, we have the person who's watched a few seasons of Grey's Anatomy - and *thinks* they are at the surgeon level. This phenomenon is called the Dunning-Krueger Effect.

In the field of psychology, the Dunning-Kruger Effect is a cognitive bias in which people with low ability at a task overestimate their ability. It is related to the cognitive bias of *illusory superiority* and comes from people's inability to recognize their lack of skill.

People who have read a few articles or books, and have limited skill in a subject, are far more likely to call themselves an expert. In this book, please be careful, and be suspicious if you find yourself thinking, 'I've heard that before.' The best way to get the most from this book is to get into the 'beginner' mindset, as if everything here is brand new.

In the military, they have a common phrase I've heard thousands of times:

"Knowing is the enemy of learning."

KNOWLEDGE VS. SKILL

I have a small online presence, but I'm amazed at how often I receive messages from people who tell me how many journal articles they've read, books they've consumed, and websites they've 'researched' on behavior.

Of course, they are all well-meaning, and many of the things I've received have been fascinating. But I noticed a trend over the years; people get addicted to information, to knowledge.

They have an insatiable appetite for information and knowledge but are very rarely able to **perform** the techniques. It took me a while to understand it, and I realized that many of these people are the ones teaching body language, people-reading, persuasion, and influence around the world. The difference between academic *knowledge* and real-world *skills* is so vast that it could be a book in and of itself.

If we took the top salespeople from every Fortune 500 company and the top 100 interrogators in the world and analyzed them, what would we discover that they had in common?

If we really were able to sit down, speak with these people, and got to know them, would they be:

1. The people who have read every book on techniques, tactics, and tricks for interrogation or sales?

OR

2. The people who have through-the-roof social skills, can read anyone they speak to, and make anyone feel incredible?

It's universally agreed that they would all be option two. Skills beat information. That's what the 6MX is all about.

This book will present you with a lot of information *and* skills. It will seem overwhelming at first but stay till the end. I'm going to show you how to learn this one step at a time, in a way that won't overwhelm you. In fact, the method I will show you at the end of this book takes about two minutes and can fit on a Post-It note.

All of these skills will culminate into one behavioral profiling tool called 'The Behavior Compass,' allowing you to develop a behavioral profile beyond what 99% of psychologists are capable of seeing in less than six minutes. You'll know more about someone's behavior and fears than their own friends and family do. I promise.

"THE 2/3 RULE"

Body language trainers around the world enjoy citing a study published in the 1970s by Albert Mehrabian.

His study suggests that 93% of interpersonal **communication** is nonverbal and that the words we use are only 7% of what's going on in a conversation.

I, and many other experts, such as Mark Bowden, Scott Rouse, Greg Hartley, and Tonya Reiman, disagree. It's a 'body language myth,' as Bowden calls it.

If you're face to face with someone and they don't speak your language, chances are you won't be able to communicate anything of substance nonverbally. This number of 93% might be a little high.

Here's the interesting part: the same university that published the study doesn't teach nonverbal communication...to anyone. If you obtain a Ph.D. from UCLA, you will average only a few minutes learning about *the importance* of nonverbal communication. This isn't that UCLA is a bad college. In fact, all universities have about the same amount of training for psychologists in nonverbal communication.

If nonverbal communication is 93% of communication, and all psychological therapy is communication, why do we spend less than .003% of the time training people in what is, apparently, so critically important?

We may never know.

Let's conservatively estimate that about 2/3 of communication is what's being said (we will delve into this later.) If the study shows us anything, it shows us that nonverbal communication is essential, regardless of what precise number we assign it. It's more than half for sure.

For simplicity's sake, we will use the 2/3 rule for this. So somewhere around 66% of communication with people is nonverbal.

But why?

THE HUMAN BRAIN

In the grand scheme of our species' time on earth, we only began talking to each other a few minutes ago. For millions of years (if not more), we didn't have language at all. Our ability to communicate with each other was nonverbal—the same way dogs communicate.

Not only did language evolve over time, so did our brains.

Our brains evolved in three fundamental parts:

- The Reptilian Brain
- The Mammalian Brain
- The Neo-Cortex

The reptilian brain was the first to form in our heads. It's also called the Basal Ganglia or brainstem. Its functions are instinctive responses, impulses, and physical sensations. It's basically what's in a snake's head—primitive, and hell bent on survival.

The next phase of our mental development was the mammalian brain. This is where we store implicit memories (we'll talk about this later), emotional experiences, feelings, and desires. This part of our brain is right between our ears. For a hundred million years or so, this part of our brain has been communicating nonverbally—it predates language by a long shot. The mammalian brain is the reason we make most of our decisions in life.

The mammalian brain reads the behaviors of other people. For millennia, this part of our brain has passed down nonverbal communication techniques to the next generation. We can pass down 'genetic memories,' and nonverbal communication is one of the pieces of 'software' that comes pre-installed in all of us. This is the reason we are born with certain nonverbal communication skills. For instance, facial expressions are pre-installed, along with hundreds of other gestures and behaviors our ancestors used to communicate with each other before we invented language. Babies smile and cry and frown all because our ancestors gave us these behaviors.

Let's examine a quick example of this brain in action. Think back to the last time you met someone, and everything went well. Their behavior was great; they were well-spoken and seemed quite pleasant. Yet, something didn't feel right, or something about the conversation didn't add up, and you just couldn't put your finger on it. It was just a 'gut feeling.'

This happened for a few reasons. First, the mammalian brain can't speak English. Actually, it can't speak any language at all. The mammalian brain deals in behavior and emotion. But it's also the part of our brain that 'reads' other people.

Using the accumulation of millions of years of training, this part of your brain is scanning other people all the time, in every conversation you have. The trouble is, the mammalian brain can't communicate what it's seeing. It would be great to get a crystal-clear explanation from it, but we can't; it deals with emotions. So, when it sees something that doesn't add up, it gives you a feeling some people might refer to as intuition. This is the reason we are unable to put our finger on precisely what we saw.

Second, there's an information barrier from the mammalian brain to the neocortex. When the mammalian brain sees something relevant, the neocortex takes all the credit, so we go backward in time to rationalize what we saw in the conversation and even fabricate memories of what took place to justify the 'gut feeling.'

When we are exposed to communication that influences us, it lights up the animal brain. It creates emotional drives to action that flow upward to the neocortex. That's when all of us, as humans, reverse-rationalize the decision and convince ourselves that it was based on logic, fact, and cold-hard science.

When we buy a product, for example, we tell ourselves we're not manipulated by commercials, ads, or other people. We think we did lots of research and continue to rationalize the decision in our neocortex that, in actuality, was made by our mammal brain in response to something that provoked a desire to buy the product in the first place.

Think of good communication as a tool. A tool that breaks through the wall between the neocortex and the mammalian brain. It creates desire, action, impulse, and emotion.

The neocortex is what makes us human. This intellectual and executive functioning part of the brain is pretty young compared to the other two parts of our brain. The neocortex is where we process logic, creativity, questions, art, music, and ponder why we exist in the first place.

We read behavior using our genetically inherited skills. The 6MX process is so effective because it capitalizes on identifying behaviors that are not only unconscious but are programmed deeply within our brain. We are learning to see with the 'human' part of our brains in order to bring what's hiding behind the mask into the light.

YOU'RE COMPETING WITH SOCIAL MEDIA

For years now, an article has been circulating the internet, suggesting that people's attention spans have been shrinking over time. People might assume that since we are increasingly inundated with marketing, popups, ads, flashy videos, and non-stop notifications, our attention span is getting shorter, but this isn't the case.

Our attention spans *aren't* shrinking. They are *evolving*. While we do get flooded with attention-grabbing material throughout our day, we don't lose attention span. Our brains learn what to focus on. It has the appearance of an attention deficit, but it's not. It's an interest deficit. I'm not saying the clinical diagnosis of ADD is non-existent, that's something else.

You might struggle to concentrate during an incredibly tedious college lecture, but the capacity to binge-watch three seasons of *Game of Thrones* is entirely within you.

Our brains are getting better at rapidly identifying something that is interesting or important.

Our brains are highly adaptive; they memorize patterns to instantly recognize when something is relevant or interesting. With this new skill that our electronics have given us, we've become selective even in conversations. Scrolling through social media and having the ability to flick away a video the moment it becomes uninteresting has resulted in the development of a hyper-screening brain.

When you're in conversations you're competing, with clickbait, cat videos, and even whatever porn that person watches, for attention. There is one single phrase I have every student write in their notebooks in my live courses:

Focus is currency.

THE 'WAIT TILL THE END' FALLACY

In sales, dating, interrogation, or whatever scenario you'd like, people tend to wait until the end of the interaction to discover the other person has objections. Interrogations sometimes last countless hours before an officer must face the reality that he's not going to get a confession. A sales professional may spend several hours talking with a customer only to find out at the end that the customer is a 'no.'

This was one of the problems I spent years addressing. The 6MX process will show you exactly how you can spot all of these objections as they happen in real-time. This will allow you to not only spot the objection but to deal with it the moment it occurs.

You'll also be able to see every hidden, concealed, and repressed disagreement your customer is experiencing, even if they aren't fully aware of it.

But it's not only negative behaviors you'll learn to spot. As you interact with people, you're going to notice every single instance they feel happy about something. You'll know, instantly, whether they're excited about a topic or interested in something you've mentioned. This is valuable insight as to what they will respond to later on in the conversation. I'll show you how to build their behavioral profile in less than six minutes, and it's a skill you can use in every conversation you have for the rest of your life...and no one will know.

THE WORD 'DECISION'

Why do *homi**cide***, *pesti**cide***, and *de**cide*** end in the same letters?

The suffix of decide is *'cide,'* which means to *'kill'* or *'cut off'* in Latin. The prefix *'de'* means *'off.'*

When we encourage people to make decisions, we are making them 'cut off' the option to do anything else. The more you see in behavior, the better positioned you will be to make this happen. To help others 'cut off' from all other choices.

SUMMARY

Human behavior matters a lot more than most people realize. In every decision and interaction, behavior takes the reins – mostly in the background and without our awareness. So much of what influences us arrives through a nonverbal channel and secretly determines how we behave.

As our brain evolved, we became human, but there's still a wild animal in there that calls the shots when it counts. When we can read behavior with clarity, the whole world changes. We know more about an interaction than anyone we know, and we can practically see the future based on someone's reaction.

In the next chapter, you're going to be shown the exact way that a true behavior profiler sees the world around them and exactly how it can legitimately change your life overnight.

CHAPTER 2

SEEING PEOPLE IN A NEW WAY

These laws won't stand up to academic scrutiny, but as we learned earlier, there's a massive difference between **research-based** and **results-based** techniques.

Sometimes research takes a while to 'discover' what has already been working for a very long time.

I created these four laws as a filter. If you practice seeing others in this way regularly, and if this is the only thing you take away from this book, your entire life *will* change. I can promise you that.

With each of the laws of behavior, try to imagine as many scenarios as possible that prove the law and illustrate it to be real, because they are very real.

One thing you will begin to see on a daily basis after learning to read behavior is that people tend to look sadder and more scared. When I first learned how to read human behavior, I thought I was doing something wrong. Everyone seemed to be hiding sadness, and I remember seeking out guidance from my mentor. We sat down to lunch one afternoon in Hawaii at the Navy golf course. He quietly explained that in Buddhism, suffering is the universal condition of *all* creatures. It turns out to be true that everyone is hiding suffering from the world around them.

We are frail creatures, and it's okay.

My entire life changed with this discovery, and I'd like to pass what I've learned on to you. This brings us to the first law of human behavior:

LAW 1: EVERYONE IS SUFFERING AND INSECURE

This might sound like doom and gloom, but it's actually something you can keep in mind next time you feel like you're faking it or that other people really do live the way they portray themselves on social media.

People are fragile creatures. A few hundred thousand years ago, we had to continually worry a lot about being social. The average tribe or group numbered about 70-150 people. If we were to appear unstable, unpredictable, weak, or even anti-social, in this small group, we stood a chance of being outcast by the group. This hurt our chances of having sex and passing our genes on to the next generation.

Since NONE of your ancestors died a virgin, you did okay! They passed down these behavioral traits to you to help you survive. The brain in your head is no more evolved than it was a couple hundred thousand years ago, so it's still running the exact same programs your ancestors did. The hard truth, however, is that we have no ability to go into our 'settings menu' and delete or stop some of these programs from running in the background of every aspect of our lives.

LAW 2: EVERYONE IS WEARING A MASK

Some people call it a persona. We present an image to the world. We have a strong, primal desire to be socially accepted by groups and people. If we didn't, we'd be outcast.

We all know people who think they don't wear a mask, and we struggle to interact with them as they typically have the thickest masks of all. This innate need to be accepted and fit in, or be social at all, is programmed into our brains so deeply that it's almost our default operating system, like a Windows or Mac OS.

Some masks are thin, some are thick, but we all have a face we present to the world. In this training, you'll not only learn how to identify the mask and remove it, but I'll also show you how to see behind that mask without anyone knowing you're doing it.

LAW 3: EVERYONE IS PRETENDING NOT TO WEAR A MASK

It would be a silly interaction if we engaged with other people and spoke about our masks all the time. This thought of 'the mask' is usually enough to make people want to leave a conversation because it sets off a series of feelings in people that range from shame to anger.

We pretend not to wear a mask because if we acted otherwise, the entire purpose of presenting ourselves to the outside world would be meaningless. The mask is meant to stay private—we all wear one, but we don't talk about it. Later in this book, I'll show you how you can talk about it and how to do it in a way that makes someone start to peel theirs off a little bit.

As we all go about our days, the mask is with us, but we'd like the mask to look as much like our face as possible. We don't want it to be visible.

LAW 4: EVERYONE IS A PRODUCT OF CHILDHOOD SUFFERING AND REWARD

We form a lot of our beliefs and behavioral patterns unconsciously. When we are about twelve, 90% of our behaviors toward other people are solidified. At the age of eighteen, it's highly unlikely that anything is going to change regarding our interpersonal behavior.

Imagine you've just gotten off work. You're driving along the highway home, and an asshole in a giant pickup truck cuts you off. After he jerks his vehicle in front of yours, he reaches out the window and flips you off.

Most of us would be upset about this. But what if you were able to see this person through the lens of the laws of behavior? What would they look like?

As you get more involved with the book, you'll be able to see people through this lens. The guy in the truck won't look like an asshole anymore. Instead, you'll see who he really is. A little boy who grew up. When he was a child, something happened (or several things did) that made him cry—an emotional experience that changed his views of the world. That little boy, who's now driving that big truck, stood in front of a mirror, or cried into a pillow, and somewhere in the recesses of his mind, a permanent belief about the world was formed. A promise was made: "I will never be hurt again. If people are scared of me, then they won't hurt me."

That little boy was hurt, and he still is. He's reacting from god-knows-what occurred in his childhood. It could have been an alcoholic mother who made fun of him, a deadbeat dad who ignored or abused him, a school bully who hurt him in front of people. We don't know what it was, but just imagining an event in your mind can help you to start seeing people through the lens of the laws of human behavior.

What about the person we all know who wants to *show you* how smart they are? No matter what you say, they respond with 'Actually...' or they want to tell you more about your own ideas. It's an annoying behavior that can rightly make anyone mad. But what if you saw the little girl whose parents made her feel inferior and stupid? What if you saw her sitting in a classroom with a teacher who made fun of her in front of the class for screwing something up?

> The world changes when these four laws
> stay in your awareness.

Have you met a person who wants to take charge of everything? Try to see the kid who felt insignificant in their home when they were little.

Have you met someone who wants to argue about everything? Try to see the child who felt they could never win anything and went through a phase where several kids in school were actually out to get him or her.

Now that you've read the four laws of behavior for the 6MX system, I have a confession to make... there are five laws, but I am saving the fifth law until we unearth a few more techniques of people reading. The fifth law sounds a bit unusual until you've been exposed to something called The Human Needs Map, which explains it.

THE FOUR LENSES TO SEEING PEOPLE

The Laws of Behavior are a lens to see people through. It changes everything.

The four ways of seeing people breaks down how we can begin to see people differently, but this can also be used to identify how someone else sees the world. So, it's not only a technique to change your perceptions, it's also a profiling tool to read behavior.

Let's take the example we used before about the person who cuts you off on your way home from work. I will illustrate the four ways of seeing people using this example. There are four phrases to identify the different lenses people view others through.

1. People are **broken**
2. People are **different**
3. People are **facts**
4. People are **reasons**

PEOPLE ARE BROKEN

These people tend to see the behaviors of others as being screwed up or stupid. They will get cut off by the guy in the truck and have an emotional response that they feel inclined to alleviate. They want to fix the situation so that they are back on 'top' of the person who cut them off. They might speed up and cut him off to show him he's not powerful or try to somehow re-establish their power and control.

In this lens, the person is *actively participating* in *resistance* against another person. They typically will also make an identity statement in their mind in response to the situation, meaning that they will take the actions personally and feel as though they have been chosen to be the target of this person's actions.

PEOPLE ARE DIFFERENT

This group of people will still have a strong emotional reaction to events and negative behaviors from other people. The difference is even though they may take it personally, they are more likely to decide *against* taking action to rectify the situation and 'correct' the other person's behavior. Even though they may fantasize about the truck running off the road into a ditch, they aren't going to make it happen.

PEOPLE ARE FACTS

We can't correct facts. When something happens like a hurricane or a flood, we know internally that we cannot change them. This is the fundamental reason we humans don't get mad at natural disasters. We may get mad at its results or the consequences of something happening, but not the hurricane itself. When something is absolute and unchangeable, we don't get mad.

One reason we do this is because when we feel anger, it's a secret desire for something to be different. Most times, it's a secret desire to change something. These people view humans as facts: unchangeable and permanent. They don't look at people in a negative way at all. They only default to assuming there's nothing that will change the person.

These people are typically much happier in contrast to the previous two because of this.

PEOPLE ARE REASONS

This is the highest level – the level at which a behavior profiler views the world.

As the truck swerves in front of them in their car, they slow down safely and increase their distance from the truck. While this happens, their mind automatically defaults to the laws of behavior. In particular, the first and fourth law.

They see the actions of others as a product of behaviors learned in childhood. Without a negative thought about the other person, they know the behavior is something all humans are capable of. The negative behaviors are a product of pain, suffering, and childhood experiences that shaped a person into who they are today.

Judgment disappears at this point. When we see through the lens of 'reasons,' everyone is human, and everyone is equally screwed up, just in different ways.

None of us would get mad at a bee if we got stung. We might be mad we got stung, but it wouldn't be focused on the creature, just the circumstance. We do this because we see the bee as a reason: it's reacting based on what evolution has shaped it to be. It is a bee – that's one of its jobs. We can do the same with humans – we go from '*that guy's an asshole*' to '*someone hurt that guy a long time ago*' or '*I wonder who made that guy feel so small and insignificant when he was younger.*''

SUMMARY

While you might have identified yourself on a lower level than you'd like, that's good news! We can't manage what we don't measure and knowing about it is step one.

When we learn to see through the lens of psychology and behavior instead of logic or bias, all of our interactions change. People are all reasons. The moment you're able to steer your thoughts back to this during interactions, the more you'll be able to pull the curtain back and see people in a light that might not be flattering, but is accurate.

In the coming chapter, we're going to dissect behavior skills and how to use a thing called The Behavioral Table of Elements (BTE) © to profile anyone you will ever meet in only minutes.

CHAPTER 3

BEHAVIOR SKILLS

You've seen a lot of body language articles out there. Some promise to deliver the secrets to 'when she's ready to be kissed' or 'sure signs he's cheating on you.' The trouble is that these articles typically all make one major mistake: The Attribution Error.

The Attribution Error is something that happens when we are told a single gesture has a singular meaning. For instance, one I see regularly is when body language teachers tell you that someone crossing their arms is deceptive, withholding, concealing, defensive, closed-off, etc. This type of thinking and training is deceptive in and of itself.

When we read behavior, context is key.

If you were in discussion with someone and they showed a tiny facial expression of disgust, we might recognize the facial expression, but the training in body language or people-reading is useless without learning how to establish the context, topic, or subject that caused the facial expression. For instance, if you saw disgust immediately after mentioning Hillary Clinton or Donald Trump, you'd immediately know a lot about the person in front of you. You'd even have a small window that shows you how they view the world.

If you're in a sales position, and you see something I call 'lip compression,' when the lips squeeze together; you'd be seeing 'withheld opinions.' However, not knowing what was being said being when you noticed the behavior makes the skill of observation next to meaningless. If you're talking to a customer, and you start going over payment terms or interest rates on payments, and they tell you it sounds good to them, but their lips compress as they nod to you, you've got work to do. Not only have you spotted a *concealed* objection that has the potential to ruin the sale, but you've also identified precisely where to take the conversation next to disarm or overcome the unconscious objection.

In a moment, we will walk you through the Behavioral Table of Elements and how to read it. Before we do that, I would like to illustrate one key concept: clusters.

The Table has been laid out in a way that resembles the Periodic Table of the Elements for two reasons:

1. I thought it looked cool and recognizable
2. It shows us that, just like the elements, they get 'added' to each other to form something

The cells in the Behavioral Table are laid out in such a way that, to form a cohesive opinion about behavior, the elements of behavior must be combined. Without context, we fail. Without clusters, we don't know much.

THE BEHAVIORAL TABLE OF ELEMENTS

I designed the Behavioral Table of Elements (BTE) over a decade ago for analyzing the behavior of prisoners overseas undergoing interrogations. It has since been hung on the FBI academy walls and is used in hundreds of police departments around the world. I wanted to develop a cohesive system that had the potential to make observations about human behavior into something that could be communicated and understood by anyone.

However, as badass as it sounds, its origins are probably more interesting…

In 2005, I was watching an episode of *The Bachelor* with my mom. We sat in my parent's study drinking wine as she introduced me to a show I'd not seen before. My mother walked me through how the show 'works,' and detailed the girls in the show she liked and the nasty qualities of the women in the show she didn't like. It was a fascinating concept. My mother then told me how one of the women was 'really sweet and honest,' and I had to interrupt. Since they had TiVo, I was able to rewind the episode and showed my mom that the 'sweet and honest' woman had lied to the Bachelor three times while they sat in the hot tub. I paused at the right moments to illustrate the deception indicators, and she was impressed by my skills (which made my night).

She said, "I wish I could just borrow your eyes to watch this show…"

That's right, she wanted to use my nearly one million dollars of training in interrogation and behavior analysis to watch *The Bachelor*. However, it intrigued me.

Later that night, as I lay in the bedroom I grew up in, I couldn't help but think of my childhood. When I was a kid, my mother had a dozen or so waterproof kids' placemats. Each placemat had educational material on it, so as I scarfed down oatmeal in the mornings, I could look at the placemat and learn the continents, the planets, the list of US Presidents, and even the capital cities of the United States.

I lay in bed, thinking, 'How can I translate all the training I have into something that can fit on a placemat?'

I spent years researching and countless hours on my knees in my living room, rearranging notecards and counter-checking against academic research to ensure I had something that was a decent attempt at getting my entire behavioral training onto a single page.

I somehow managed to become a Microsoft Excel nerd during this process, and figured out how to piece it all together.

Finally, I had a product. I sent it to my mom, and she was impressed…and seriously confused.

"Okay," I thought. 'I can make this right.' So, I built ONE MORE 'placemat' containing instructions on how to read it.

It was done.

You can download the entire
Behavioral Table of Elements for free by visiting
www.chasehughes.com/behavior-profiling

The Table is something you can simply keep on your phone, iPad, or wherever you can see it often. I promise I'm not going to have you going through this thing cell-by-cell, but let me introduce you to how it works.

As the world-first behavior profiling tool, The Behavioral Table of Elements (BTE) was designed to have applications everywhere, from an overseas interrogation room to a first date. The Table not only allows advanced, standardized analysis of behavior, but it also assists in training operators in recognizing behavior signals and seeing the crucial elements *everyone else* misses during a conversation.

THE CELL KEY

- **Symbol:** Each cell's unique symbol for abbreviation
- **Name:** Brief description of the behavior
- **Confirming Gestures:** Confirm the original, intended meaning of the gesture or behavior
- **Amplifying Gestures:** Add meaning to the original, intended meaning of the behavior
- **Microphysiological:** Small physiological indicators to measure the severity/intensity of the behavior
- **Variable Factors:** How many variations of this single behavior have been identified
- **Cultural Prevalence:** Whether a certain culture is more/less likely to perform a behavior

- **Sexual Propensity:** Whether males or females are more/less likely to perform a behavior

- **Gesture Type:** Which of the 4 behavior types this behavior is: Closed, Open, Aggressive, or Unsure

- **Conflicting Behaviors:** Behaviors that indicate conflict with behavior's intended meaning

- **Body Region:** Which body part or region is most often involved with the behavior

- **Deception Rating Scale (DRS):** Likelihood of stress/deception on a 1-4 scale

- **Deception Timeframe:** Whether the behavior is likely to be seen Before (B), During (D), or After (A) a response is given to a question

ARCHITECTURE

The BTE is laid out so that the top of the head is at the top of the Table. The feet and lower body are lower on the Table. From left to right, the BTE indicates the least stressful/deceptive behaviors to most stressful/deceptive behaviors. The bottom two rows contain behaviors that are verbal or take place outside the body or with objects.

COLORS

- **Red letters** may show up on a non-stressful cell. This means that if this behavior is seen in the same period as a behavior that contains a 4.0 on the DRS, the behavior with red letters automatically becomes a 4.0 on the DRS

- **Blue Letters** in cells mean that temperature will increase this behavior in all humans. In cold environments, these behaviors can be lowered in point-value or overlooked

- **Green Background:** are the least stressful behaviors on the chart

- **Blue background:** Variable, in that they can present in different values, such as breathing rate – fast or slow

- **Turquoise Cells:** Indicate facial expressions and microexpressions

- **Tan Cells:** Indicate slight discomfort and stress

- **Yellow Cells:** Indicate higher discomfort behaviors

- **Grey Cells:** The behaviors with the highest level of stress (4.0)

DECEPTION

Deception is rated per question-and-answer scenario. If a subject's behaviors tally up to more than 11 points on the Deception Rating Scale during the entire question and answer period, deception is highly likely.

The Behavioral Table of Elements is a lengthy study, and I made a promise I wouldn't have you going through the entire Behavioral Table.

What we are going to focus on in the coming chapters are the most powerful and reliable behavioral indicators I've discovered in my 15,000 hours of interviews, interrogation analysis, and research. I can assure you that once you get these basics translated from the information-stage to the skill-stage, everything changes. You'll start seeing the 'human matrix' immediately, even after finishing this next chapter.

SUMMARY

If you haven't downloaded your free copy,
you can do so at:
www.chasehughes.com/6mxbookresources

Now that you're at least familiar with the anatomy and navigation of the BTE, you'll be able to reference it as long as you'd like throughout this book, watching The Bachelor, or even performing job interviews.

KNOWLEDGE CHECK

1. How many points are needed to grade a response or statement as 'likely deceptive'?

2. What does a green background represent in a cell?

3. What do blue letters signify on the BTE?

CHAPTER 4

THE EYES

We spend most of our time in conversations making eye-contact. In fact, experts have even suggested that you make eye contact 50% of the time while speaking and 70% of the time while listening. That's a lot of eye contact.

I'll dispense with the old trope about the eyes being 'windows to the soul' and such. Let's break down the results-based techniques for seeing behind the mask, and I'll show you how much the human body reveals during a conversation.

Since we are making eye contact most of the time, even if we're addressing a group of people, we must we pay attention to them. They reveal so much information that if you *only* studied the behavior of the human eye, you'd still be privy to more information than anyone else in the room.

BLINK RATE

How often we blink reveals a lot about our internal state of mind.

In most conversations, the typical blink rate in conversations is somewhere around nine times per minute. Blink rate at twelve-per-minute is average for most of us and can go up to 20 or so without much happening.

In conversations and stressful situations, our blink rate can be upwards of seventy times in a minute! For instance, when I took the Math portion of my SAT exams, my blink rate was probably in the high seventies.

When we are calm, focused, interested, or relaxed, our blink rate can decrease to as little as three times per minute. When you watched a movie that captivated your focus and attention, your blink rate was probably very slow. When you had a conversation with someone that was interesting or fascinating, your blink rate was probably the same as it was during the good movie you watched.

The interesting point about this is that we aren't aware of this shift in behavior. It's never in our conscious awareness, and it's extremely difficult to control.

Since this is an unconscious behavior that occurs without our awareness, it's a reliable indicator of stress, discomfort, interest, and focus.

Almost all the behaviors you'll be learning about are like this—unconscious, hard to control and occur outside our normal awareness.

The good news is that you don't have to count blinks per minute. If you'd like to, here's the formula to do so. And this works even if you're speaking to large groups of people, or the situation is one-on-one:

Whether it is with people in the audience or the single person in front of you, as you make eye-contact, count how many times you see them blink in a roughly fifteen-second timespan. Multiply the blinks times 4, and you will have the person's blink rate. If you're speaking to a large group of people, you'll be making eye contact with several of them. As your eyes move from person to person, count how many blinks you see in that fifteen-second window, and do the same thing; multiply the blinks you saw times four. You'll have an average blink rate of the *entire* audience. You'll know immediately if they are interested and focused, or stressed and bored. This invaluable information can direct your speeches, training, lectures, sales...you name it.

If you don't want to spend your time in conversations counting blinks like a behavior nerd, here's what I recommend. When you start a conversation, observe the person's blink rate, and determine whether it is fast, average, or slow. With this information in mind, as the conversation progresses, you'll be able to **notice changes** in the blink rate.

While you're speaking with someone, if you mention something that captivates their focus and interest, you'll be surprised at how easy it is to see the shift from average or fast to slow. It's easier to spot than you think.

If you're in a conversation and you see the blink rate speed up, you've received an immediate indicator of stress or disagreement. Depending on the context, you'll be able to identify a stress-point. For instance, you're in a business negotiation, and as you mention a detail about the contracts someone signed, you see their blink rate spike from 12 per minute to somewhere around 60 per minute. That contract, and the mention of it, is causing an adverse reaction. This vital information is an insight you've gained immediately at that moment. Of course, you would have to have knowledge of the contract to determine the context of the behavior, whether it is a stress reaction or some kind of fear about losing the negotiation.

I train legal teams for what is now called 'Trial Consulting.' One of the many indicators I teach to legal teams, whether for deposition, jury selection, or cross-examination, is blink rate. If you're an attorney speaking to a jury, and you want to get them completely focused on a story or narrative, you need to be looking for slow blink rates. The jurors who exhibit no change in blink rate will show you that you need to do a little more work in getting them on board. If you wanted the jury to experience a stressful/emotional recount of a crime, you'd be looking for jurors who exhibited faster blink rates. This indicator alone could spell the difference in a courtroom between embarrassment and success. You'd know the jurors who were on your side and the ones you needed to 'work on.'

In any conversation you have, start noticing this behavioral indicator. As the conversation begins, make note of the person's blink rate. Is it normal, fast, or slow? Most of the time, your goal will be to not only *cause* the person to exhibit a slow blink rate but to identify *what causes changes* in their blink rate. Did it speed up? Then **your immediate goal is to identify what caused the change and act on it**. In sales, you can pre-empt objections. For legal teams, you can immediately shift course to whatever subject or topic caused the jurors blink rates to lower earlier in the conversation, or you can discuss something right away that makes them agree with you before proceeding.

Identifying the blink rate is much easier than you think. If you bring up a few videos of celebrities getting grilled on sensitive issues, you'll see how easy it is to spot the immediate shifts in the blink rate.

I am obsessive about notes and records. I have stacks of journals locked away with research and notes in them. When I performed an analysis of an interrogation or interview, I would use a simple symbol code to take notes on what I observed. One of the requirements, especially if I was taking notes live in an interview, was that I could not allow the note-taking system to be deciphered.

I call these *Compass Notes*. They earned this name because I built a non-decodable system for building a human behavior profile without them knowing what my notes said. A person's entire secret behavioral profile, including their hidden fears and insecurities, all fit within a small circle that I called a Behavior Compass. We will get to this toward the end of the book, but it looks like this:

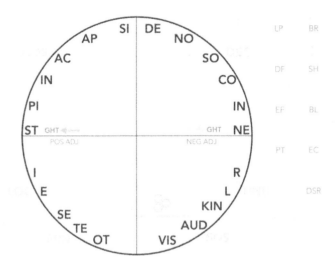

For the blink rate, the notes look like this:

1. Add a simple '*Br*' to a place inside the Behavior Compass
2. I observe the blink rate as the conversation begins
3. If the blink rate is normal, I will simply put a hyphen '-' next to '*Br*'
4. If it is fast, I'll add an up arrow
5. If it is slow, I'll add a down arrow
6. When a change occurs (faster or slower), I will add that arrow to my notes
7. If I was able to determine what caused the change, I will circle the arrow

GESTURAL HEMISPHERIC TENDENCY (GHT)

There is a lot of information circulating the interwebs and cop television shows that is inaccurate. Even popular TV shows like *CSI* have fallen victim to this belief. In this technique, if a person looked a specific way, someone could tell if they were accessing certain types of memories, fabricated memories, and even outright deception.

This was proven to be unreliable, but eventually, experts agreed there were certain behavioral *habits* regarding eye-movements that *were* reliable.

Our eyes move to access our memories, and they move when we think of certain types of memories in specific ways. If you asked someone about a car crash they experienced or an ex-spouse they disdain, you're likely to see their eyes move a certain way when they speak, say, to the left.

If you asked them about a fantastic vacation or a really good movie they saw, you'd see the eyes typically move in the other direction. Not only will they access positive and negative memories using different directional glances, but they will also almost always use that same-side hand to gesture as they speak about the positive or negative events.

If you're in sales, and a person is recounting how they just got back from an amazing trip they took to Belize, and looks to their right, they will also likely gesture with that hand when they speak about it. If you were to ask them why they didn't like the previous company they were dealing with, they would look in the opposite direction as they recall all of the reasons they are unhappy with the other company.

Everyone is different, and I've never seen a strong correlation between where someone looks and whether they are right or left-handed.

Within the first 60 seconds of a conversation, you'll be able to identify which side of the body the person uses to discuss positive information. All of us move our eyes to send our mental 'file clerk' into the brain to retrieve data.

This method is a great technique to reveal a person's mental preferences for **which side of the body they use and access to get positive and negative recall of information**, but let's unpack how to turn this into a behavioral tactic.

It's a rainy morning. You're the lead salesperson at a car dealership, and you've just been introduced to a new customer who's interested in buying a pickup truck. You ask him about his life, and he begins recounting the horrible experience he had last time he bought a truck. As he starts to recount the horrible experience, his eyes move to his left, and he begins a series of small gestures with his left hand. You've immediately identified that he is what is called 'right-positive' by nothing more than elimination. If the left side is for accessing negative information, the right side will be what he uses for positive information.

As you begin to close the deal, you can now lean to your right (his left side) and gesture with your right hand (also on his left side) while you describe the benefits of owning this new pickup truck. You've physically moved a bit to his right side and forced his body and eyes to start moving in the direction of his positive memories and associations.

To simplify this, they look a certain way when they recall positive information; then you move that way and gesture that way as you close the sale.

If I'm speaking with someone and I see them look to their right as they talk about anything that they view as positive, fun, enjoyable, interesting, or good, I'm going to move that direction when it's time to close the deal.

The bonus of identifying GHT is that you also know which side they associate with and access to retrieve negative information. If you would like to make a subject or topic viewed in a more negative light, all you need to do is move in that direction. For instance, you could be talking about a competitor. Suppose you're in psychotherapy and dealing with a patient who needs to change their behavior. In that case, you can describe the consequences of not changing their behavior while adjusting your posture and leaning in the negatively associated direction.

GHT is a powerful tool. You can go online today, and almost any video with people in it will show you how easily you can profile GHT.

Compass Notes:

To take notes in meetings about GHT, I will simply write 'ght' followed by 'lp' or 'rp'; those standing for left-positive and right-positive.

My notes on GHT might look like this: ght-lp. It's simple, and no one will be able to comprehend the notes.

EYE HOME

Whenever you speak with someone, you'll notice that accessing their memories and thoughts will cause them to look in a certain direction. Think of the human face like a clock for a moment. If your customer has spent an hour answering your questions and every time you asked them for information, their eyes went to the right (their three o'clock), that would be their 'Eye Home'.

Eye home is **where we *typically* look to access memories** and recall information. Sometimes, distinct types of information can cause people to look in different directions on their 'clock'.

I didn't believe much in this until I sat with a good friend and world-leading behavior expert, Greg Hartley. The man has written *ten* books on behavior analysis and body language, so when he spoke, I listened. Here's how you can prove this to yourself right now:

Think of the sixth word of your favorite song. Your eyes moved, didn't they? Awesome! That proves you're human. Now, think of the closest shopping center to your home. What is the third store from the right when you're standing at the front? Your eyes moved again to recall this memory. Since one of them was a word-bank memory, and the other was most likely a visual memory, your eyes may have moved in different directions to retrieve information for each of these memories.

How's all this important?

When you asked your client all those questions, and determined their 'Eye Home' was at three o'clock, you were able to quickly form what is called a baseline. **A baseline is**

how someone behaves under normal conditions and circumstances.

If you know this client's Eye Home is at three o'clock, and then when you ask them what their credit score is, their eyes dart over to nine o'clock before they answer, you've seen something no one else will ever notice. You've seen a *change* in behavior. This deviation from their baseline is indicative of potential deception, doubt, or fabrication.

Take a look at this fictitious transcript from a jury-selection panel:

Attorney: "Can you please tell us your name?"

Juror: "Matilda Thompson." (eyes don't move because this information isn't hard for her to recall. It doesn't cause her to need her 'file clerk' to go back and pull data from memory.)

Attorney: "Thank you. And have you lived in this area for a long time?"

Juror: (looks to her nine o'clock position before answering) "I'd say it's been about nine years, yes."

Attorney: "How would you describe your feelings about the police here in the city?"

Juror: (eyes dart to the nine o'clock position before answering) "I think they do a great job, actually. I've never had any issues with them, personally."

Attorney: "Thank you. Could you tell us about your job? Says here you work in customer service."

Juror: "Yes. What would you like to know?"

Attorney: "Could you tell us how many people you deal with on a normal day?"

Juror: (eyes jut over to nine o'clock position before answering) "Oh, I would have to say about forty or fifty people come through the office every day."

Attorney: "Thanks. I have a more personal question for you here if that's okay, Miss Thompson. Have you ever been a victim of domestic violence?"

Juror: (eyes move to three o'clock position, then downward before answering) "Uh, no. No. I haven't."

In this imaginary case, the attorney missed a crucial indicator. This woman's potentially deceptive comment about domestic violence could cost him (and his client) the case.

Eye Home is important to establish early in a conversation, as we are making eye contact with people, and our eyes move a lot while we speak. When you can establish where someone generally looks for information, you will be able to spot the moments that this doesn't add up.

If someone's Eye Home is two o'clock, for example, keep in mind that it may be in a different location if you're asking them about something that requires a lot of visual memory or emotional memory.

They may look in a different direction for visual information. As the conversation progresses, continue to collect data points for where you see their eyes move. After only a few moments of speaking, you'll be able to establish their baseline and will be prepared to spot critical deviations from it.

One note of caution:
Strong emotional memories make our eyes move downward.

I've seen this across all cultures. If you're speaking with someone about an emotional event or asking them to recall emotional memories, you'll regularly see this downward eye movement.

Compass Notes:

From the center of the Behavior Compass, I will simply draw a small arrow to show which direction the person looks to access memories. Their Eye Home will be established on the Compass to come back to it for future meetings or conversations.

SHUTTER SPEED

Blink-rate identifies how often the eyes blink; Shutter Speed identifies how fast they blink.

Shutter speed refers to the speed of a camera shutter. In behavior profiling, it refers to the speed of the eyelid. When we blink, we reveal more than just blink rate. Changes in the speed of the eyelid can indicate lots of information.

Shutter speed is a measurement of fear.

Think of an animal that has a reputation for being fearful. A chihuahua might come to mind. In mammals, because of evolution, our eyelids will speed up to minimize the amount of time that we can't see an approaching predator. The greater the degree of fear an animal is experiencing, the more the animal is concerned with an approaching predator.

In an attempt to keep the eyes open as much as possible, the eyelids involuntarily speed up. Speed, when it comes to behavior, almost always equals fear.

In humans, if we experience fear about something, our eyelids will do the same thing as the chihuahua; they will close and open more quickly. In a conversation, if you see a change in shutter speed, it can indicate either the presence of or reduction of fear.

As fear takes hold in the body, you will see an immediate increase in how fast the eyelids are closing and opening.

Side Note:
You've got a new understanding that fear causes the body to move faster, not just the eyelids. With this in mind, think about the mammalian brain in the person you're speaking to. It's unconsciously reading your behavior. To communicate well, we should be sending the right signals to this part of the brain. A good rule of thumb to follow is never to move faster than you would if you were in a swimming pool. This keeps any of the unconscious fear signals from broadcasting during a conversation.

PUPIL DILATION

In conversation, we spend most of our time making eye contact. How often do you notice the size of pupils? Probably not often. Our pupils change in response to lighting conditions, but they also respond to **visual stimuli, emotional reactions, and arousal**.

Since we aren't aware of our own pupil size, and the constriction or dilation of them is outside our conscious control, this makes it an exceptionally reliable unconscious behavior.

Suppose we are having conversations in a location where the lights aren't changing. In that case, we can assume that the pupils' movement (the constriction and dilation) is a psychological response instead of a physical one.

First, our pupils respond rapidly to threats. If someone were to burst into the room as you're reading this and start shouting, your pupils would dilate (get bigger) as much as possible. Our bodies do this in response to threats because of our history. If we are about to be attacked, our pupils enlarge to let in the maximum amount of light, allowing us to see everything better to facilitate fighting or an escape from the potential threat.

The pupils also respond to psychological stimuli.

When we are attracted to someone, our pupils will dilate as we look at them. When I teach interrogation courses, I show police officers how to display photos to suspects to observe the pupillary response to them. If a suspect's pupils dilate while observing a photo of a bloody crime scene, for example, I've got a good idea of how this person feels about the results of the crime.

When we see or hear something that we really like, our pupils will dilate. Things we dislike will cause our pupils to constrict.

Scientist Eckhard Hess pioneered the art of what he termed 'pupillometry.' He performed a series of experiments that gave us this foundational body of knowledge about pupil dilation and animal imprinting.

When babies are first born, their pupils will dilate when they look at their parents. As humans, when we look at a person with dilated pupils, we are more likely to find them attractive. However, if you're out in the bright sun, don't be discouraged if the pupils you see are constricted and small. Anytime the lighting is bright, we can ignore pupil sizes in conversations, as the bright light overrides the ability to see any fluctuations in the pupils of whomever you're speaking with.

In sales, you might see a pupil dilation response to something you're showing to a customer. This is noteworthy. Likewise, you might see pupil constriction in response to something, exposing their immediate disagreement.

Not all pupils are equally visible. People with lighter colored irises will be a lot easier to spot. This nonverbal behavior is something that I recommend trying in conversations to get the hang of. Not only will you be able to do it automatically after just a few days of practice, but you'll also be able to make much faster assessments of someone's agreement or disagreement.

CONFIRMATION GLANCES

A confirmation glance is something we all tend to do occasionally. Some people do it more often than others.

When you are speaking with more than one person, you can see confirmation glances when a person briefly looks at the third party for 'confirmation.' This typically occurs just before or just after they speak. They will make eye contact with you as you ask a question or make a remark and briefly look at the other party just before they speak.

This glance lets you know that they are **confirming their opinion with the other party** or that they are nonverbally checking the other party's approval. If you see the glance before they speak, it's likely that the person they looked at is the decision-maker and can be persuaded.

If you see them look at the other party after they speak, you can assume the person they looked at is still the decision-maker and has the final say.

The confirmation glance is simply a way to determine who's in charge, who makes the decisions, and who you will ultimately need to persuade to adopt your ideas.

When I teach law firms about this behavior, I show them how this works in the courtroom. A witness on the stand may glance at someone in the courtroom after they speak, and it could mean a major red flag or that you need to talk to this other person. In juries, the jurors will typically select 'decision-makers' before the end of the first day. You will see the juror's confirmation glances go toward decision-makers any time a fact or turning point in the case is discussed in the courtroom.

In interrogations, a confirmation glance has a new meaning as well. If an interrogator is interviewing two suspects, and one of them looks at the other *before* speaking, this behavior flags potential deception. If there are two interviewers and one suspect, deception potential is seen when the confirmation glance takes place *after* the person answers. For example, interviewer A asks the suspect a question. The suspect answers, then briefly glances at the other interrogator/interviewer *afterward* to ensure both parties believe their story.

This behavior is culturally universal and can be seen anywhere humans talk to each other. Try watching a celebrity get interviewed on a show and see whether their glances tend toward the host or to the audience, and you'll know which one they want to please the most.

THE EYEBROW FLASH

Make an angry facial expression.

Did you feel what your eyebrows did? They pulled downward and together. As primates, we communicated with our bodies and faces for millennia. If we wanted to show another primate that we were **non-threatening, friendly, and open**, we would make a movement with our face above the tall grass to prevent conflict.

The eyebrow flash shows on our face as the opposite of anger. Our eyebrows go upward and apart. Think back to the last time you met someone you were excited to see. Those millions of years of genetic memories activated to show that you were friendly. As you greeted them with enthusiasm or introduced yourself, your eyebrows 'flashed' upward to show them you were not a threat.

This isn't something we do consciously. So many of us are completely unaware of the behavior of our eyebrows. As an experiment, try introducing yourself to someone today and perform an eyebrow flash. There's about a ninety percent chance the person you do this to will return the same eyebrow flash. The only difference is that their body did it completely unconsciously! We tend to exhibit a lot of the same behaviors that primates do unconsciously.

We've all seen the articles or the online videos that tell us that our bodies play a role in our psychology. Some say if we make facial expressions of happiness, we actually start to make happiness chemicals in the brain. If we sit up straight when we feel down, our mood will begin to shift. On an internal level, we are all pretty aware of this. The movement of our bodies can create moods. Moods create movement (body language), and movement creates moods. The theory works in reverse. But what does it have to do with the eyebrow flash?

In the first few minutes of conversation, you're already able to apply everything you've learned up to this chapter. You can profile all eye movements, and you have The Laws of Behavior to use as a lens to see through. But in the first few seconds of an interaction, you can perform an eyebrow flash.

When someone returns the eyebrow flash unconsciously, they've begun to exhibit behaviors of compliance, non-threatening, and open body language. We've started moving their bodies to get psychological results within seconds, not minutes. This is the first step to something I developed for intelligence work and our persuasion courses called 'behavioral entrainment' – wherein we guide the person into a gradually increasing number of compliant behaviors as the conversation progresses. You'll learn more about this in the coming chapters.

Compass Notes:

> The Eyebrow Flash can be denoted by a simple '*Ef*' followed by a checkmark to denote the person responded to your Eyebrow Flash at the beginning of the conversation. To annotate that they responded with an Eyebrow Flash to a particular topic, your Compass Notes may look like this: '*Ef-interest rate*'

SUMMARY

The eyes communicate (reveal) so much information, but only if you have the skill to identify it. Since we've been using our eyes to communicate for millennia, they know what they are doing so much that they are on autopilot.

If you studied nothing more than the eyes and made this your only skill, you'd still be better than 95% of people in the world.

Keep in mind, reading people is not just about *seeing* these behaviors. It's about **watching for changes and identifying the cause** of that change. Next, let's look at the face, since we are already making eye contact all the time, and I'll show you a few things you might have never seen or heard of before that expose a lot more than most people are comfortable with.

CHAPTER 5

THE FACE

We humans make a lot of eye contact. Even in countries where eye contact isn't as prevalent as it is in Western countries, they still spend a lot of time looking at the eyes. The next part of the body we look at the most is the face. A person typically glances at the face 11 times per minute in conversations.

The most impactful researcher in facial movement science was Dr. Paul Eckman. Eckman traveled to the jungles' depths to seek out tribes who had never been exposed to outside human contact to verify that facial movements and facial expressions are universal.

We truly are born with the same facial expressions and nonverbal communication strategies, and Dr. Eckman proved it. His groundbreaking book, *Unmasking the Face*, paved the way for modern researchers in behavior science.

In this chapter, I will only introduce you to the absolutely essential elements of the face that you will need to know to read people. I'll list the behavioral indicators in order of importance (according to me).

LIP COMPRESSION

When a person squeezes their lips together, they are performing one of the first ways humans learn how to say 'no.' When we don't want to breastfeed, we close our lips.

If I were to give you the most accurate two-word description of what this behavior means, it is '**withheld opinions**.' Lips compress to withhold.

In sales, if a customer is speaking to you and you see their lips compress right after they say, 'Yeah, that sounds pretty good…', you know you've got work to do. There's a hidden or concealed objection waiting for you at the end of the sale if you don't deal with it now.

What if you asked a close friend how they like their new job, and their response was, 'Oh, it's great!' followed by a lip compression. If you try this now, you can feel that you've done this in the past when you were withholding opinions. We all do it.

In the courtroom, when you see lip compression in a jury, you've got work to do. If you're deposing someone, and they answer a question followed by lip compression, you know something is being held back.

At the beginning of the book, I mentioned the importance of context. This is no exception. It's critical that you're able to identify the *cause* of the lip compression. Otherwise, spotting the behavior is next to useless.

If you are speaking about the price of a product or service when you see Lip Compression, that detail is what you need to make note of. You can deal with the objection in the moment or keep the information in your pocket till the end of the sale when you start closing the deal, and then bring it up and overcome it before they can raise the objection.

Many times, people we deal with will have unconscious objections or objections they may never verbalize at all. The ability to spot these indicators is essential. You may never hear the objections spoken out loud. When you lose the sale or fail to get compliance, you (and probably the customer) will be unaware of the real reason that the deal didn't happen. The lips can show us objections and disagreement that are totally outside the customer's conscious awareness.

Compass Notes:

Lip Compression could be annotated by noting 'Lc' followed by what topic you believe caused it. For instance, in jury selection, it might look like this: '*Lc – police officers*'

OBJECT INSERTION

This is one to be on the lookout for. Object insertion means something is being put into the mouth. It could be a pencil, the end of a pen, a woman's hair, or even the lips. Once something passes the barrier of the teeth, it qualifies as object insertion.

This behavior is usually indicative of a **need for reassurance**. Regardless of the situation, if you see this behavior in a conversation, it should be a red flag, notifying you that you have work to do.

When we see this behavior, we know the person most likely needs reassurance. Our priority here is to identify the subject matter or topic the person reacted to with object insertion.

From here, you have the option to immediately provide some kind of reassurance about the issue or save the information and preemptively address the issue later—providing the needed comfort as their desire to be reassured comes to a head.

Compass Notes:
As before, annotate using 'Oi' followed by the topic or subject that preceded/caused it.

TRUE VS. FALSE FACIAL EXPRESSIONS

In conversations, it's a valuable skill to know when a facial expression of disagreement, happiness, or even surprise is not the real thing. For example, in negotiations, false disagreement in the face will show you that you've made an offer they are likely to accept, even if the other party says otherwise.

In the courtroom, a witness pretends to smile as they talk about how happy their home life is, as they make a confirmation glance at someone in the courtroom. You're able to immediately identify the expression as false, allowing you to sharpen your questions around the topic.

Regardless of the environment, our faces tend to betray us when we express ourselves to others. We've been making facial expressions and sending nonverbal cues for a hundred million years or so, but we've only begun speaking recently, in the grand scheme of things.

Since our nonverbal (mammalian) brain has been making genuine facial expressions and passing behaviors down through our genes for millennia, it's relatively good at getting the expressions to look a certain way on our face. **Genuine facial expressions are automatic** when we feel emotions. False facial expressions come from a completely different part of our brain. This fact provides us with two main clues to spotting false social expressions on the human faces we see every day:

THE STOP VS. FADE OF EXPRESSIONS

False facial expressions will drop off the face instead of fading. When real facial expressions are made in the brain, they come from our animal brain. False expressions come from our neocortex, the 'human' part of our brains. The neocortex is so inexperienced at the art of facial expressions that it will stop the expression after it makes it. Genuine facial expressions are chemically based. The chemicals wear off in our bodies, and the genuine expressions will fade off the face, not just stop suddenly.

> **Genuine facial expressions fade. False facial expressions will suddenly go away.**

THE ASYMMETRY OF FALSE EXPRESSIONS

Since the neocortex is so inexperienced at making facial expressions, it lacks the precision the mammalian brain does to tighten the facial muscles equally. The mammalian brain has millions of years of practice at expressions, and our **authentic facial expressions are almost always symmetrical**.

False expressions are likely to have more muscular tension in the face on one side than the other. You will see the asymmetry when someone is telling you that they agree when they don't.

There is one notable exception to this: the contempt facial expression. Contempt is when we feel defiance, disregard, or disdain for someone. This true facial expression resembles a half-faced smile or sneer that is more prominent on one side of the face than the other.

THE ARTIFICIAL SMILE

An artificial smile isn't deceptive. We often see articles referencing 'fake' smiles, referring to them as being artificial or deceptive. This isn't the case.

Humans are social animals, and much of how we get along in life depends on our social skills. A smile to others means we are friendly. We smile at people all the time to be polite, with no intent to deceive, only to get along and show respect.

The artificial smile is easy to spot. It's something you can scroll through social media right now and find. In genuine smiles, the upper half of the face is very involved.

The cheeks raise and show what some experts call 'crow's feet' in the outer corner of the eyes. Regardless of our age, those crow's feet show up when we smile. Even babies display this when smiling genuinely. One study even showed that people who smiled genuinely in their college yearbooks were happier decades later than those who displayed false smiles.

You should be able to look at someone who is smiling, cover up the entire lower half of the face, and still see that they are smiling. If someone is wearing a ninja mask, for example, you should be able to tell if the smile is genuine immediately.

For smiles, watch the eyes.

NOSTRIL FLARING

In behavior science, this behavior is called 'wing dilation.' Nostril flaring occurs mostly as a response to an increase of adrenaline in the body. As the adrenaline levels increase, **the brain needs more oxygen**.

Since we are social creatures, when our body needs air, we don't open our mouths wide and pull in a considerable volume of air, especially if we're trying to hide the emotion.

The nostrils will flare due to the need for oxygen, and the need for oxygen is caused by adrenaline. The adrenaline can be a product of intense feelings of excitement, happiness, or even anger.

It's up to you to determine the context. If you're in a sales situation and you're going over how much someone will have to pay in order to use your service, and you see lip compression and nostril-flaring, you can assume this isn't a good sign.

All emotions leave clues, and it's our job to figure out not whodunnit, but *whatdunnit.*

If you're a police interrogator, and a suspect hears their name has been cleared, and you observe nostril flaring behavior, you can rightly assume this adrenaline is anticipatory excitement.

Learning how to spot this behavior doesn't take much time at all, and since we are already looking at the face most of the time, you won't have to divert your attention away from the conversation to spot this behavior.

Finally, nostril-flaring can indicate attraction. If you're speaking to someone and see this while you are speaking, this can indicate attraction. The evolutionary cause of this has its roots in our desire to smell the breath of someone we find attractive or see as a potential partner.

Compass Notes:

Annotate Nostril-Flaring with a simple 'Nf'. If someone's nostrils flared the moment they made eye contact, I would write, '*Nf @ Ec*'

HUSHING

Another behavior we see children do all the time is hushing. They accidentally drop the F-bomb in front of their parents for the first time, and their hand instinctively comes up to cover their mouth. As we grow up, we don't outgrow this impulse; we figure out ways to mask it a bit.

Any behavior that obscures the mouth from your view is considered to be hushing behavior. Hushing can indicate a few things...

When listening, hushing can indicate **a person wants to stay quiet out of respect**. They might casually bring their hand to their mouth as they listen. Context is important.

Mouth-covering and facial touching have proven to be one of the most reliable *potential* deception indicators, but remember there are no behaviors that indicate deception, only stress. Imagine you're speaking to someone, and the moment you mention interest rates on a loan, they tell you that sounds good to them, but they also touch their face as they say it. You've got work to do.

In the courtroom, jurors, witnesses, and even the judge will exhibit facial-touching and hushing gestures **when a topic creates internal stress**.

Suppose you're explaining something to someone that they may object to and you see mouth-covering (hushing) behavior. In that case, it is a noteworthy indicator that could definitely indicate that you will need to explain further or ask the person if they have any reservations or questions about the issue.

Compass Notes:

This behavior could spell disaster for many professionals, but parents should look for it too. Annotate this in notes using a simple '*Hu*' followed by the relevant causal subject. For instance, it could be written as, '*Hu – credit score*'.

SUMMARY

The face now enters as our first major source of information about how we are doing in a conversation. Stress, agreement, concealment, and even deception show themselves more often than you realize. When you learn to read the face, you get some serious leverage.

Moving further down, the next chapter will show you only the most exposing and critical behaviors you can easily learn to spot that reveal stuff people would much rather stay hidden.

KNOWLEDGE CHECK

1. What is the most likely meaning of lip compression?

2. What does it mean if someone places a pen into their mouth during a negotiation?

3. If you see someone scratch their nose in a way that covers the mouth when they are discussing their relationship history, is this a good sign or a potential bad sign?

CHAPTER 6

THE BODY

Over the years of developing the 6MX process, I've concentrated the research and training to include only the most reliable and most common behaviors to spot in order to gain the most accurate information about who you're communicating with.

The body's behavior is just as reliable as the face, but we spend less time in conversation looking at the body. This section of the 6MX contains the essential behaviors that can be observed on occasion and others that you will observe in your peripheral vision while making eye contact.

CROSSED ARMS

There are countless articles online illustrating all the varied meanings of people who cross their arms. However, most are unreliable. If you observe someone crossing their arms, the causes and reasons can be so varied that it becomes an inaccurate assessment.

If you observe arm-crossing behavior, **ignore it.**

There are two exceptions to this:

1. When the palms are in contact with the body, this is a **self-hug**. It is a reassuring/pacifying behavior that can indicate a need for reassurance or insecurity. This behavior is not arm crossing.

2. If the person is making fists instead of merely crossing their arms, this is significant. It can indicate **anger, restraint, or serious disagreement**.

If you see a simple 'normal' looking arm-cross, ignore the behavior with one exception. The fingers of the person you're observing should be taken into account. The tension in the fingers can illustrate the psychology of the person. **Relaxed fingers** show us that this person is generally relaxed, and that the behavior is simply an extension of that. If the **fingers are curled and dig into the arm, you are seeing discomfort, stress, or disagreement**. This finger movement is called digital flexion, and will be covered later in more detail.

NOTE: We tend to think in terms of still images when learning behavior and body language. This is a critical error that many make as they learn the art of people-reading. As you imagine each of these behaviors, picture the movement from one behavior to another. For instance, instead of memorizing what the curled fingers mean with the arm-cross, imagine a moving picture of what that behavior looks like; the fingers going from relaxed to curled on the arm. Now you can place the behavior with the context that created it. In all of behavior analysis, we are watching for changes and movement, not still images.

Compass Notes:
Annotate using *'Acc'*.

GENITAL PROTECTION

Men and women will perform different actions that qualify as genital protection.

Men will perform a behavior known as the 'Fig Leaf,' women will perform something called a 'single arm-wrap.' Both of these behaviors communicate the same internal feelings:

Either **vulnerable, threatened,** or **insecure.**

THE FIG LEAF

Men's hands will retract toward the genitals, eventually ending up being held in front of the genitals together. In a standing position, we have all seen this behavior, a man standing upright with both hands held together in front of their groin. In a seated position, this same behavior can be observed, with one or two hands covering the genitals. The movement of this behavior is what you are going to be looking for.

Imagine a conversation with someone. A man's hands rest comfortably on his legs. As a topic is mentioned, the hand(s) slide backward toward the groin area, covering the genitals.

In this case, the movement is what tips us off to the context that created the emotion. We see the hand move towards the genitals and immediately identify the topic being discussed that caused the movement.

SCENARIO:

You're a therapist speaking to a patient with depression, and as you mention their relationship with their mother, their hands move backward, settling in front of the genitals. You know immediately that you need to ask questions about this.

SCENARIO:

You're in a high-stakes business negotiation, and as you talk about the terms, you mention that a new board member will be appointed to the company. As you say the new board member's name, you observe the retreat of the hands toward the genitals.

You could be seeing **vulnerability, insecurity, or the feeling of being threatened** by these topics.

THE SINGLE-ARM WRAP

Women will exhibit the single arm wrap when experiencing the same feelings.

SCENARIO:

Imagine you're a hiring manager at a financial firm. You sit down to interview a young woman, and everything is going well. As you ask her about why she left her previous employer, she says, "Everything was fine there. I just needed a change of scenery." As she began her statement, you noticed her **arm fold over her lower abdomen, and her hand gently grasp her forearm**. You've identified genital protection. You know you have work to do here.

SCENARIO:

Now imagine you're a doctor. A female patient comes in and is complaining of headaches. While gathering her medical history, you ask her about feelings of depression or self-harm. As she denies having those feelings, she crosses her arm across her belly, and her hand comes to rest on the opposite forearm.

Genital protection is woven into our entire psychology. While we no longer have to protect our reproductive organs from attacks by tigers and lions, the instinct to do so is still alive and well within us. Internal feelings are on public display.

Compass Notes:

Annotate both the Fig Leaf and Single-Arm Wrap using 'Gp' for genital protection, followed by the topic you believe to be the cause of the behavior.

DIGITAL EXTENTION

Our fingers reveal a lot about how we feel. Typically, the further a body part is from the head, the harder it is to control during stress and elatedness.

Digital extension is a behavior that reveals **comfort, agreement, relaxation, and focus**. In other words, it's good when you see it.

Digital extension is a small movement of the fingers away from the palm. The fingers are moving from a curled position (not a fist) to a less-curled position. They are relaxing. This behavior can be seen from your peripheral vision and doesn't take long to learn. Simply watching a few online videos can show you exactly how common this behavior is and how easy it will be to spot.

In most seated conversations, hands are placed on the table or within your view. If they aren't in your view, you can obviously ignore the need to profile the hands. But since the hands are visible most of the time, they serve as a reliable barometer of how well the conversation is progressing.

Compass Notes:

Use a simple '*De*' followed by the topic when you observe Digital Extension.

SCENARIO:

You're a senior executive and involved in negotiations with another company for a massive deal. Amid the tensions, you've agreed to a meeting with the other company's representatives. As you go through your list of points, you notice digital extension across the table when you make your initial pricing offer. This is a good sign, as you've discovered the number is favorable to the other party.

SCENARIO:

While checking in to your flight, you observe digital extension in the airline employee as you mention the topic of cocktails. This discovery lets you know that the topic is favorable, so you decide to elaborate on it and wind up being upgraded to First-Class.

Digital extension is an excellent barometer for conversations. Whenever you see this behavior, take special note of what is being discussed. This is something you may want to bring back up at the end of the conversation when it's time to ask the person for a favor.

Over the course of a conversation, negotiation, or discussion with anyone, digital extension alerts you to every detail that causes the person to relax and pay attention.

DIGITAL FLEXION

Digital flexion is a negative behavior. It can illustrate **disagreement, doubt, anger, stress, and even fear**. Since you will already be on the lookout for digital extension, digital flexion will be equally easy to spot.

The behavior has the reverse appearance of digital extension, wherein the fingers curl inward toward the palm. This behavior is not someone making a fist. It is a gradual, and most times, subtle, behavior that can involve minimal movement of the fingers.

Context is crucial. When you see digital flexion, its meaning is unknown until you're able to understand the topics, subjects, or events that likely created the behavior.

Compass Notes:

Use *Df* followed by the behavior.

SCENARIO:

In a sales office, a customer shows digital flexion the very same moment you mention a warranty. You immediately identify this and ask them if they have any questions about the warranty by saying, "I realize there's a whole lot here. This warranty thing is especially confusing sometimes. Did you have any concerns about it?"

SCENARIO:

It's Friday night, and you've been dragged into a speed-dating event with friends. You sit down at a table with a man who is charming and friendly. As you make a casual joke about 'criminal records,' you spot strong digital flexion. He hands you his number at the end of the evening. Instead of calling him right away, you search online and discover a felony assault charge. Yikes.

Digital flexion isn't a sure-fire indicator of deception or even concealment, but it is something to look for. Now that you've been trained, you'll know that once you see it, it becomes a relevant data point, and you know to look for others. Any time you see digital flexion, identify the context, and consider it a valuable data point to either deal with in the moment or contrast to future behaviors.

FIDGETING

Fidgeting is written about in body language articles all over. Fidgeting happens when a person repetitively makes small movements with the feet and hands. This behavior typically serves no purpose but can alert us to a few possibilities of its meaning.

Fidgeting occurs when we have increased adrenaline or when our brain is under-stimulated (bored) and is attempting to keep our mind active.

A good rule of thumb from body language expert Joe Navarro is that '**all repetitive behavior is self-soothing**.'

If you observe this behavior, it's likely the person you're speaking with is either excited or bored, but it could be neither. Once you've taken the context into account and observed the other visible behaviors, you'll be able to determine the meaning of the behavior.

Fidgeting serves us only as a data point among many and is not a behavior that I would recommend you pay close attention to, but it is worth noting when you see it. Make note of the context anytime you see this behavior.

Compass Notes:

Use 'Fi' followed by what you think caused the behavior.

FEET HONESTY

Our feet tell a story about intent. If you approach a group of people who are talking, you'll notice the feet pointing toward the person in the group who has the most attention.

This will typically be either the leader of that group or someone who is most socially connected to them all. The direction feet are pointed can tell us quite a bit, and the good news is you don't have to stare at them during a conversation.

The feet are furthest from the head. They are far more likely to betray our intent nonverbally than our other body parts, which live closer to the brain and are easier for us to manage.

In any conversation, make an occasional note of which direction feet are pointed. If they are pointed at you, that's a great sign. If they move from pointing at you to pointing at an exit, this might indicate their desire to leave the conversation. **Feet broadcast intent and focus.**

When speaking to multiple people, note where feet are pointed as well. If you're talking to two people, and one of them generally point to the other person, you've probably identified the decision-maker in the group.

Feet will also be the first body part to display fidgeting, although we are less likely to observe it if we're making eye contact or seated at a table

ARMS BEHIND BACK

This behavior is similar to the arm-cross. It's widely written about and often misunderstood. Our species once walked on all fours. Since we did this, our soft bellies were protected from predators by the hard ground below us. Now that we are upright creatures who can take selfies, we walk around with our abdomens exposed, the rib cage not protecting this area.

Behavior expert Mark Bowden has coined the term 'truth plane' to describe this area. People who speak with exposed palms just above waist-level and expose their abdomens are more likely to be trusted by others.

When someone places their hands behind their back, it doesn't mean much more than they **don't feel threatened**. They are showing us that they have no need to protect the abdomen whatsoever.

We also see this behavior in authority figures who unconsciously do this to illustrate their confidence. In all reality, however, it simply means that someone feels just fine.

There is one exception to this. If the person has their arms behind their back and one hand is clasping the arm behind the back, this is indicative of **self-restraint**. This gesture can indicate someone is restraining either due to anger or out of fear they will do something they would rather not. In the anger scenario, you can see this in courtrooms as a suspect stands to listen to a jury's verdict. In the fear scenario, you can see this when someone who doesn't want to bungee-jump is peering at the equipment looming near the edge of the platform.

HANDEDNESS

Identifying someone's dominant hand is something we can all do. From seeing which pocket they carry a wallet in to simply watching them write something, we can all identify clues to spot someone's dominant hand.

Our dominant hand, and that side of the body, plays a significant role in our behavior and reveal a lot more than most people think.

In our courses for police and government, I teach people how to predict violent behavior before it happens. One of the most common indicators of pre-violence is a behavior called 'dominant leg retreat.' Picture yourself standing normally. If you were to get into a fighting stance or about to hit a punching bag, your dominant foot would draw backward to prepare your body for action.

In police encounters, and especially when someone is attempting to conceal their intent to attack, this backward leg movement is very subtle, sometimes moving only a few inches backward.

After decades of watching human behavior, I've discovered something: When a person experiences strong disagreement with you, their dominant shoulder will move backward just like the foot does before a fight occurs.

If you're seated, imagine the person across from you pulling their **dominant shoulder away from you**. Most of the time, it will be a very subtle movement, only an inch or two backward. But this behavior is a reliable indicator that the person is experiencing a **strong negative reaction to something** in the conversation.

This behavior is easy to spot without staring at the shoulders, and it may save you a lot of money and time once you're able to spot it. Here is the method that I teach interrogators and law firms around the country:

When you identify that someone is left or right-handed, place an imaginary red circle in front of that shoulder. It only takes a second to do this. Now that you've done this, even if the circle vanishes, your brain is still primed to watch for movement in that area of the person's body. If you see the shoulder move away from you, you will be able to see it a lot easier.

Compass Notes:
A simple *'Rh'* or *'Lh'* will do when filling out the compass for this.

BREATHING LOCATION

If you watch a baby sleeping, you'll always see one thing they all have in common: they breathe into their abdomens. Their bellies will rise and fall.

Ours do the same when we sleep. In fact, anytime we are fully relaxed, we will breathe into our abdomen. Most of us, especially in new social situations, will breathe into our chest area.

Chest breathing can indicate someone is in disagreement, but this behavior can be the default behavior of people as well. What is important about identifying breathing location early in the conversation is that it enables us to identify when it changes to a different area.

If I see someone breathing into their chests in an interrogation room and notice a **shift to abdominal breathing**, this becomes a good data point.

If I'm speaking with someone who is relaxed and breathing into their abdomen, that's great. But if I see a shift in breathing location and they **suddenly start breathing into their chest**, this can indicate something is off.

If you're looking at someone's face, you'll be able to tell if their chest is rising and falling. If their chest isn't rising and falling, you can assume they are breathing into their abdomen.

Compass Notes:

Make note of when you see shifts in this behavior. Note a quick '*Ab*' for abdominal breathing or '*Cb*' for chest breathing, followed by the topic or what was mentioned that likely caused the behavior.

SCENARIO:

You're on a date. The conversation is going well, and you casually mention reading an article about shoplifting. As you do, your date's breathing immediately shifts from **relaxed, abdominal breathing to chest breathing**. While this may not indicate your date is a serial shoplifter, you've established a data point that will help you make much better decisions about the future of the date, where the conversation will go, and possibly whether you need to run.

SCENARIO:

You are selling life insurance. After speaking with a client for a few minutes, you note that they are a chest-breather by nature. But as you begin talking about renting an RV for a family vacation, you see the person's breathing shift into their abdomen. This gives you valuable information about what's important to this person and allows you to discuss the benefits of the insurance policy in a way the client will appreciate.

Breathing location is important, but only when we see a *change*.

SHOULDER MOVEMENT

THE SHOULDER SHRUG

When we shrug our shoulders, it can indicate either **submission, an apology, or a lack of information**.

When both shoulders go up, our body communicates that we are sorry. If someone asks if you have any idea when a flight is leaving from a gate at the airport, this gesture would probably be exactly what you did if you didn't know.

Our shoulders also come up when we are **fearful**. With our fear of large cats still in us from long ago, our shoulders raise to protect the neck. All fear behaviors will protect arteries and blood vessels in some way. This behavior also serves to make us smaller and can reveal someone's fear of situations or people. When I train police, an indicator I teach them to look for on domestic violence calls is shoulder shrugging. Does the victim show raised shoulders in the presence of the abuser? This can help an officer see what's really going on behind the scenes.

This expression is also a way to show **deference to authority** figures. Subordinates may approach a boss with shoulders raised, or a child who wants something from their parents may do this to show deference as well.

In general, people who are experiencing fear of any kind will raise their shoulders. **People with anxiety will carry their shoulders high** most of the time until they fully relax.

When you see **shoulders dropping or relaxing, this is a wonderful sign** that you've made someone comfortable and accepting.

In conversations, look for this behavior. Not only will the raising of shoulders show you when the person is feeling fearful or uncertain, but it will also expose all the conversational topics and discussion points they are comfortable with and interested in.

Compass Notes:

When taking notes on this, abbreviate using *Sh.* Raised shoulders should have an up arrow, circled if you're able to identify the cause of the behavior. And lowering shoulders should be a down arrow, circled for the same reason.

THE SINGLE-SIDED SHRUG

The single-sided shrug occurs when someone quickly raises one shoulder. This differs from the general shoulder shrug in that it communicates a whole different message. This behavior displays a lack of confidence in what's being said.

It doesn't always imply someone is lying, but it can certainly show where someone **has little faith in the statement they are making**.

Imagine asking a friend how they like their new job. As they say, 'It's great!' one-shoulder spikes up. We know they don't fully believe in the accuracy of their statement.

SCENARIO:

As a newly minted salesperson at a car dealership, you're speaking with a couple about buying a new SUV. When you ask them if a particular model is the one they are looking for, you see the woman's shoulder rise quickly as she says 'yes.' Right away, you understand that you will likely have to explore a few more models and see if they like any of them.

SCENARIO:

You're on a date with someone you met online. The moment they tell you they would like to go on a second date, you observe a single-sided shrug. You've either got work to do or better luck next time.

BARRIER BEHAVIOR

Countries erect barriers, and so do we. Most of the time, this is an unconscious behavior. The table between you and a client is completely clear, then they take a sip of water and set their glass between you and them. This is a barrier.

We place objects between ourselves and others when we feel **a need to distance, conceal, or protect ourselves** from the conversation or the person.

Barriers can take many forms. For instance, someone buttoning their jacket suddenly in a meeting could be a barrier behavior. A woman pulling a shirt closed as she speaks to someone can be a barrier gesture. Even something as small as placing a phone between you and the other person can be a barrier.

It's important if we're communicating to **eliminate these** as much as possible on our end. Unbutton the jacket, move that water glass, loosen the tie, and scoot that notepad a little to the side. Our removal of barriers, even our own arms, can show transparency and honesty, allowing the other person's subconscious to process the information we give them with openness and more trust.

There are two things to cover regarding barrier behaviors in the people we speak to.

1. **Identification**
   a. As accurately as you can, identify the things taking place that have caused discomfort. If you see the placement of a barrier, ask yourself, 'What were we just speaking about before this took place?'
   b. You may need to backtrack in the conversation and address the issue, or simply decide not to mention it again.
2. **Removal**
   a. If you see a barrier placed, try to **get them to remove it**. For instance, if I observe someone placing a glass between them and me on a table, I may decide to show them something on my phone, making them have to move the glass to the side.

Compass Notes:

Use *Bar* to annotate this shift in behavior. Make note of what conversation topic you see this with.

HAND TO CHEST

We tend to touch our chests while we express something we feel emotionally sincere about. This behavior can indicate someone **feels strongly about an issue or topic**, and this knowledge can help you steer the conversation.

If you see this behavior suddenly in conversation, make note of the topic of discussion.

HYGIENIC BEHAVIOR

Any behavior that has the intention of improving physical appearance is considered hygienic.

These behaviors include:
- Lip-licking
- Adjusting hair
- Picking lint from clothing
- Adjusting to a more upright posture
- Smoothing wrinkles on clothing
- Adjusting clothing (such as a jacket or tie)

These behaviors can reveal a lot, depending on the context of the situation.

In interrogations, these behaviors will most often be seen before someone begins to speak. In the subconscious, this is designed to improve physical appearance and **help you believe the story** they are telling.

In sales conversations, this can reveal the moments someone is **becoming excited** about the product's potential uses or offer they are hearing about. This can also show us when someone is preparing to discuss something they are proud of, such as an accomplishment or achievement.

In regular conversations, however, this behavior can indicate **arousal, attraction, and interest**. Not all of it is romantic, though. People do this regularly in conversations with people they have just met and people they admire.

Unless you're an interrogator, or you're speaking to someone who may be deceptive, this is **usually a good sign**.

SUMMARY

The body moves a lot but the movements you'll be able to spot won't take long to master, and will give you an edge to see well into the subconscious of anyone you speak to. Keep in mind; this is only the beginning.

In the coming chapters, we're going to investigate very detailed scenarios where you'll see this in action, and you'll see precisely how to employ each one of the techniques you're now learning, in REAL-TIME.

Let's talk about lying and deception.

CHAPTER 7

DECEPTION DETECTION AND STRESS

There are no behaviors that directly indicate deception or lying. What we are looking for is discomfort, stress, and uncertainty when someone is speaking. In this regard, you're not only learning how to detect when deception is likely in conversations, but you're also learning how to detect stress. This skill reveals all kinds of internal emotions, whether you're in sales, medicine, negotiations, or any other situation where you speak to humans.

Becoming a stress-detector has tremendous benefits. You can start to see where disagreement, discomfort, and uncertainty creep into the mind of anyone you speak to. When you see these behaviors, you will be able to identify the precise moment they occur and what was being discussed that might have caused it.

In this chapter, we are going to cover verbal 'deception' indicators and nonverbal indicators. The verbal indicators are written to address deception, but remember to read through them with the intent of applying them universally.

ABOUT LYING

No machine or human can 'detect' lies. Even the polygraph is a machine that measures only stress responses. One of the reasons they are inadmissible in court cases is the fundamental unreliability of the machine. They are prone to subjective interpretation, manipulation, and are even biased against truth-tellers.

To get proficient at determining the likelihood of deception, you must read behaviors in groups and clusters. When we see a single data point, we must obtain another before making any kind of determination about the presence of deception in someone's statement. One of the reasons I designed the Behavioral Table of Elements to resemble the Periodic Table of Elements, aside from the fact that it looks cool, was to show that they come together to form things, just like elements. Behavior is the same in that we need to combine multiple data points to create a cohesive opinion about the interaction.

We are all affected in conversations of all kinds by something called the 'truth bias.' This phenomenon suggests that when we like someone, even just a little, our brains will make a decision, without our knowledge, to see only truth. Deceptive indicators and warnings are deleted from the memory of experiences with people. Our brains are working to do the right thing, and when we interact with someone we like, our brains will seek confirmation of this and ignore anything that conflicts with it.

We see this in extreme situations where a husband is cheating on his spouse. Everyone in the neighborhood knows about it except for his spouse. She has ignored fundamental indicators of deception and bad behavior simply due to a firmly held belief or desire to believe that the relationship is still solid and going well.

We can be affected by truth bias in the courtroom, in sales, and in almost any conversation we have. It's not just something spouses and interrogators deal with. Something as small as looking like someone, sharing the same first name, or even being the same race as someone can trigger this truth bias. While there's no vaccine to prevent this from happening, knowing about it can help. Before you enter into an important conversation, examine the situation. Determine if you're likely to suffer from the truth bias and keep it in mind during the interaction. This won't prevent it, but it can certainly limit the influence of the bias on you.

Let's walk through the verbal deception indicators.

HESITANCY

Hesitancy occurs in two forms. In one form, there is an **unusual pause** before a person answers a question. How do we know what's unusual? We only measure how unusual the pause is based on how they have responded to all the other questions in this conversation.

The second form hesitancy takes is a direct repetition of the question. If you asked someone, "What's the reason you decided to do that?" and their response is, "What's the reason I decided to do that...?"—this is hesitancy. The person has echoed the entire question back before answering. This behavior is designed to buy time and provide room for the person to prepare an answer to the question.

However, if someone simply repeats a part of the question, it's most likely for clarification, not buying time. For instance, if you asked the same question, "What's the reason you decided to do that?" and their response is simply, "The reason?...Well...," this is simply a partial repetition of the question for clarification, and does not qualify as hesitancy.

PSYCHOLOGICAL DISTANCING

When someone speaks about something they feel guilty about, they will soften the severity of the crime and distance themselves (with words) from the object of the question.

In police work, criminals will use words to describe crimes that are less revolting or severe.

Kill = hurt
Steal = take
Rape = have sex with
Molest = interfere with / touch
Assault = hit
Shoot = harm
Stab = hurt

People also do this in business, referring to negative actions in the workplace with less severity than an innocent person. When questioning innocent people, they will typically have no problem using the specific 'harsh' word to describe an occurrence of something. Guilty people will tend to soften how bad it sounds.

People will also do this with names. Criminals are less likely to use the name of victims, instead referring to them as he or she, or 'the woman.' In the workplace, employees will do the same for people they either disdain or may have victimized.

Consider this statement you may have heard before:

> "I did not have sexual relations
> with that woman…"

In this phrase, we see two instances of psychological distancing. Sex has become 'sexual relations,' and the name of the subject of the sentence, 'Monica,' has been omitted. Only after this distancing phrase was the name of the subject used, and only after a pause.

When I train interrogation teams, one vital piece of advice that I always offer is that your language should do this when you question someone. There are seven specific tasks an interrogator must accomplish to get the job done. One of them is to '**Minimize the Seriousness of the Situation**.' If you ever need to question someone, never use harsh or criminal words to describe the event or action. Always soften the severity. Suspects have a mental tendency to assign blame, dismiss how severe the crime is, and rationalize their actions. One key job of interrogators is to help them do just that.

RISING PITCH

The tone of our voices tends to rise when we lie.

As stress creates adrenaline in our bodies, it also tightens the neck's muscles around the vocal cords. A deceptive statement will likely sound **higher pitched than the rest of the conversation**.

This deception-indicating behavior is easy to notice, but it won't sound like you might think. As I was first trained in this, I imagined Dennis the Menace lying to Mr. Wilson about the baseball flying through his living room window. Sadly, I discovered it's not that dramatic. The tone will increase only slightly in contrast to the other statements in the conversation.

SCENARIO:

You've been interviewing a new hire for your company. The moment you asked about why they left their previous employer, the pitch of their voice goes up. Everything else looked entirely believable, but you decide to call the previous employer and discover they were stealing from the company. Crisis averted. You're a hero...sort of.

INCREASED SPEED

Liars will increase the speed of potentially deceptive statements. This happens unconsciously, like all the other indicators. This typically has roots in one of two reasons in the subconscious mind.

Firstly, the brain is stressed out. If the person delivers the statement as fast as possible, they will **minimize the time** they are experiencing stress. The speed will differ from the rest of the conversation.

Secondly, the person being deceptive will speed up their answer to **avoid being interrupted**. If they pause, their brain views this as an opportunity for you to interject and question certain aspects of the statement

SCENARIO:

In a business merger discussion, the CEO of one business speeds up when speaking about the company's integrity and how they have been forthright in submitting all the requested paperwork. A week later, the Securities Exchange Commission (SEC) announces they are investigating the company for insider trading. (Try watching videos of Enron staff make similar statements.)

NON-ANSWERS

If a person responds to a question in any way that doesn't answer your question, it is considered a non-answer. We'll be coming back to this a few times to illustrate how this combines with other deception indicators to increase the DRS (Deception Rating Scale) number of the behaviors.

PRONOUN ABSENCE

When we speak, we use all kinds of pronouns. It's built into the fabric of our language. **Deceptive statements will contain fewer pronouns** than our normal speech and may be completely devoid of pronouns altogether.

Technical manuals typically don't contain pronouns. If you bought a new washing machine and read the instruction manual, I'd be willing to bet you'd find no pronouns in there.

Somehow, in the subconscious, our brains view this lack of pronouns as highly technical or recall untrue events with fewer pronouns because we didn't actually experience an event. Whatever the reason, deceptive statements are far less likely to contain pronouns.

Imagine asking someone what they did last night, and their answer is, "Well, left the house at about nine. Went to the bar and had like six or seven drinks, stopped at the store on the way home, got a six-pack, got home at like eleven, and played on my X-Box until about 2 AM."

Something's missing. You guessed it. Pronouns are all missing from the story. While deceptive statements may not be this dramatic, you will definitely be able to notice when the pronouns are spoken less often. James Pennebaker's book, The Secret Life of Pronouns, describes this and many other fascinating phenomena about how we speak and write.

SCENARIO:

You're speaking to a co-worker about their recent vacation. As they describe the short trip to Miami, you notice there are almost no pronouns in their description. You note this, and only a week later, discover they were interviewing for a job in NYC, not sunbathing in Miami.

RESUME STATEMENTS

Many of us get defensive if we're questioned about something we didn't do. However, most of us would simply deny having committed the offense if we were innocent. A frequent tool unconsciously used by deceptive individuals is called the resume statement.

After being questioned, they will respond to the interviewer with a long list of reasons why they would never do such a thing and provide you with a resume of sorts. This details out the **reasons they are a good person** who's honest, kind, caring, and full of integrity. People who frequently speak about their integrity may be, preemptively, giving resume statements to everyone they encounter to remove doubt and sometimes get them out feelings of guilt or shame.

SCENARIO:

You're a senior interrogator. You've been tasked to interview a suspect in a sexual assault case against a minor. You ask the suspect where they were at the time the victim stated the crime took place, and this is the response you receive:

"I've volunteered to coach that softball team for over seven years. I have a Master's in Psychology; I know what inappropriate touching would do to a kid. Not only do I respect people in my life, but I've also been teaching Sunday School at Riverside Baptist for the last four years."

This is a resume statement. But consider this: did it answer your question? Nope. In fact, in this example, we have a non-answer statement, two instances of psychological distancing, and a resume statement.

Total score (not including nonverbal responses): 16 on the Deception Rating Scale (DRS)

NON-CONTRACTIONS

We know our brains default to the most logical and technical language possible to deceive others or spin a tale to make sure it sounds highly believable. If you go back to that washing machine manual you imagined earlier; you're also not going to see contracted words in there. Where you would speak to someone casually and say, "Don't use chemicals to clean the washing machine." The manual would remove that contraction and say, "Do not use chemicals to clean the washing machine."

This technical language is not something people decide to speak with on purpose (or consciously); it's something the brain defaults to regularly when lying. The reasons for this are still up for debate, but we do know it happens.

Don't = Do not
Can't = Can not
Wouldn't = Would not
Shouldn't = Should not

Consider the following statement: "I did not have sexual relations with that woman…"

If the former president routinely spoke this way, we could discount this as non-deceptive since this is his normal behavior. Luckily, we can access thousands of hours of him speaking. This isn't his baseline behavior, so it becomes a 4 on the DRS here. With the two other instances of psychological distancing, the statement becomes a 12 on the DRS, alerting us to likely deception. This isn't even including *nonverbal* behaviors.

The good news is that if we make these little mistakes when speaking, they tend to always tally up to numbers less than 11 on the DRS. Some people will use many of these 'deception indicators' in their everyday speech. Their scores still stay below the 11 mark.

QUESTION REVERSAL

If you ask someone a question and they ask the question (or a similar question) back to you in defiance or indignance, this is question reversal.

If you asked someone, "What were you up to Monday evening?" and their response is, "What were you up to Monday evening?!" we've got an interesting data point.

What makes this even more interesting is that their response was not an answer to your question, so it qualifies as a non-answer statement. This makes almost all question reversals an 8 on the DRS.

AMBIGUITY

Ambiguity simply means the answer a person gives us is not fully functional as an answer.

If you asked someone in a business setting, "John, what were you doing after hours in the office at around 9 PM on Saturday?"

The ambiguous answer might sound something like, "Well, I usually come in to check emails."

This one is easy for us to get tripped up on. If someone uses these phrases, our brains, being experts at filling in gaps, will assume they answered the question and move on. Even worse, our brain notices the ambiguity gap, and then we ask a question that allows them to escape completely. If we got the response above and replied to John with, "So, you just checked your email?", we've provided him with a perfect escape, and all he has to do in response is say a simple, 'yep.' This gives us little room for further deception detection.

Furthermore, John's answer is not a direct answer to our question, making it a non-answer statement.

POLITENESS

Good manners don't mean deception. In this case, we are looking for a **sudden rise in the respect** the person shows the interviewer.

I had a concierge interrogation case in Los Angeles, where I interviewed someone about stolen money. He came into the room and addressed me as 'dude' and 'bro' throughout the first twenty minutes of our conversation. When I broached the question asking him if any of the other employees would have seen him take any of the money, or if one of the security cameras would have shown him taking money, his response was priceless:

"Oh, no. No sir. Absolutely not, sir. I mean, that kind of thing is not something I would do, Mr. Hughes."

This was a drastic deviation in his baseline behavior for dealing with me. The politeness spiked in response to the question about the actual event. Go back to his statement (copied word-for-word) and see if you can spot some other deception indicators in it.

OVER APOLOGIES

When we hear a **spike in apologetic speech** and behavior, we see something unusual for the person we're speaking with.

For example, if you're speaking with someone, and you hear this after asking a pointed question, you will have a strong indication of potential deception:

"What did you guys do on Thursday evening again?"

"I'm sorry. I don't know how I can possibly recall everything you want. I apologize; my memory isn't perfect. I don't know what else you want. I'm sorry."

MINI- CONFESSIONS

Our need to confess is almost hard-wired. As we feel an increasing sense of guilt about something, our need to confess, or 'get it off our chest,' also rises. The human need for confession -and the desire to release our troubles to someone else - goes back ages. Some religions even have specific outlets for this, such as Confession in church.

The second reason this may occur is still rooted in **the need to confess our sins** but also serves to derail the interviewer.

For example, in a police interrogation, a suspect may confess to a smaller crime in order to appear honest, derail the interviewer, and fulfill the need to confess. These small confessions are typically unrelated to the original event in question. If you hear small confessions, it's easy to get side-tracked and begin a whole new line of questioning based on this mini-confession. Don't. The mini confession will still be there at the end of the conversation. Your best course of action is to stay on track and calmly explain the mini-confession is no big deal and not what you're after at all.

SCENARIO:

You are serving the government as an FBI Agent. You are interviewing a suspect for a homicide investigation when they suddenly say, "I didn't have anything to do with that, but I've been meaning to tell someone that I have nineteen grams of heroin in the trunk of my car. It's parked right outside." That's a lot of heroin. Enough to make the news. It's exciting, and makes you want to go search the car immediately. However, you stay the course and continue your line of questioning by dismissing the confession as 'no big deal' and reassuring the suspect that you're not in the drug business. After the suspect realizes you have no intent on latching onto the smaller confession, and they see it as 'no big deal,' they are much more likely to confess to the larger event if they were involved. Our display of comfort and acceptance for all the other things they mentioned, leads to gradually ramped up comfort levels with larger confessions.

SCENARIO:

You're casually looking for a recipe you texted your partner on their phone. You see a deleted conversation from someone named 'Nicole' that you don't recognize. You walk the phone over to your partner and ask about the conversation and hear the following: "Oh. Yeah. That's someone from work. It's nothing. But I have been meaning to tell you something. A few weeks ago, I downloaded a dating app and chatted with a few people. I thought it was a social networking app, and I deleted it afterward."

You dodge the mini confession immediately and dismiss it as nothing, knowing it will still be there when the conversation is over. After they see that the mini-confession didn't work, your partner confesses to even more inappropriate actions with people at work.

EXCLUSIONS

Exclusions are the behaviors we see all the time in politics. Politicians muttering phrases such as, 'to the best of my knowledge,' 'as far as I recall,' and 'if memory serves…', are so normal we don't pay much attention.

Exclusions **remove you from the original answer by creating a caveat** that allows escape from anything definitive. These include the following:

- As far as I know
- To the best of my knowledge
- As I recall
- If memory serves
- As far as I am aware
- As far as I've been made aware of

These statements are stock-in-trade for politicians. We hear them daily on the news as well. However, if you're going to ask anyone a question, you must be careful about what question is asked before you announce that you've observed exclusion statements.

If someone asked you if your neighbor four houses down was selling drugs, you might rightly say, "Not to the best of my knowledge." But if someone asked you if you were selling drugs, you'd be quite suspicious if you said the same phrase.

If you're ever grading someone on the deception scale for exclusions, be sure the question is something you can reasonably assume the person knows.

Exclusions require that the suspect has reasonable knowledge about the event in question.

CHRONOLOGY

We tell most of our stories chronologically. However, if we're being questioned about an emotional event or one of our days where something significant occurred, **we will tend to lead with the emotional event**.

If you were in a car accident on Wednesday, and someone asks you, 'What happened on Wednesday?' you'll likely respond by talking about the accident. We start our stories with action, movement, and emotionally charged events.

When you hear a recollection after asking a question that involves a timed sequence that includes unnecessary detail and follows a detailed timeline, this is likely to be deception. The exception to this is if the person is asked to provide a chronological recall of events. If we ask someone to walk us through an event from the beginning, we can hardly judge them as being deceptive.

We've all made up some serious stories before. Most of us were kids, but some adults still do it. As we made up the stories, we added in details, rehearsed the lie until we had the entire thing memorized and packaged into a perfect narrative.

There's one problem, though. When we memorize something and rehearse it dozens of times, we get good at retelling it. How many times have you said the alphabet? Ten thousand? More? So, we have our story memorized to the point of recalling the alphabet. But what if someone asked you to say the alphabet backward? No matter how many times we rehearse something forwards, we will still have an extremely difficult time saying it backward.

Truthful events can be recalled in reverse. You can recall any event in your life backward. Even now, you can think in reverse without much difficulty to what you were doing at this time yesterday.

If we spot chronological stories that sound like they may be deceptive with too many details, we can ask someone to recall the events in reverse.

CONFIRMATION GLANCE

We look around at other people all the time. But if we do it at certain times, it can indicate quite a bit about our psychology and our relationship to the people we look at.

A confirmation glance, as mentioned earlier, is where a person **glances at a friend before** telling a story or glances at another **interviewer after telling a story**. These are the only two times they are a 4.0 on the DRS.

If you're with a co-worker and speaking to someone, you'll see this glance if the person maintains eye contact with you and glances back to your co-worker after they finish speaking.

If you're talking to two people, you'll be able to see one of them glance at the other just before the story/answer begins.

SCENARIO:

Having been promoted to Sales Manager at a real-estate company, you have been asked to speak to a reluctant man who has concerns about buying a home. You sit down with the man and his wife to see what's going on. The moment you ask if they are ready to buy a house, the man immediately looks at his wife before answering. You've confirmed she is likely the decision-maker, and tailor your conversation to better adapt to her communication style and desires. The home sells.

PRE-SWALLOW MOVEMENT

Just as we begin to swallow, the throat visibly moves upward. Try it now. Place your hand on your neck, and you'll feel the upward movement of the trachea as you prepare to swallow.

When people feel a sense of stress or anxiety, you will see a slight rise in this area of the throat. Anxiety associated with deception not only increases saliva production, but also causes a sensation in the throat called Globus Pharyngeus.

You'll most often see this behavior while you're asking a question. As the person realizes the severity or consequences of the question, their bodily response in the throat will be immediate.

SCENARIO:

You are a medical doctor. A patient comes into the office and asks for a prescription for a controlled substance. During your question asking them if they've seen other healthcare providers for this issue; their throat (trachea) raises almost an inch. You spot the behavior and immediately call the pharmacy they asked for the medication to be delivered to. You're able to confirm they've received several scripts for this medication this week alone.

SINGLE-SIDED SHRUG

We see this behavior all the time. When we speak with people, they will raise one of their shoulders as they explain something. This, like all the other behaviors, doesn't indicate deception on its own.

A single-sided shrug indicates someone most likely **lacks confidence in what they are saying**.

If you were speaking to a close friend and asked how they like their new job, and you saw this behavior as they said, 'It's great!' you'd know they might not like the job so much.

However, if you're in a high-ticket sales situation; and you see this as you ask the client if they feel good with the deal, you've got problems. As you notice this behavior, you instantly know you have some work to do. You can choose to address the issue right away or ask them about their concerns later. Either way, you know ahead of time instead of waiting till the end.

THROAT CLASPING

In any situation, we need to identify the context to understand behavior. If we can spot behaviors, and we know exactly what they all mean, that's still only half the battle.

If someone you're speaking with touches their neck or throat, this can strongly indicate a **self-soothing or pacifying behavior**. The hand does not have to rise and wrap around the neck. Any contact with the neck can be illustrative of doubt or a need for reassurance.

When you observe throat-clasping behavior, identify the context. If there is a point in the conversation, you can identify that caused it, that means you can overcome the doubt or uncertainty the person may be feeling there in the moment.

HUSHING

We inherit a lot from our ancestors. All of the nonverbal behaviors we have are either ways to signal other humans or protect ourselves from large predators.

These behaviors are so ingrained that we don't grow out of them. The hushing behavior is simply defined as any behavior that obscures the person's mouth from your view. Whether it's a cough, a nose-scratch, or someone directly covering their mouth, this is hushing behavior.

Imagine a child accidentally dropping the F-bomb in front of their parents for the first time. We all instinctively picture the kid reaching up to cover their mouth. We do this because that's what we would do in the same situation. This is so ingrained in us that our behaviors are compulsive.

Unlike with clothes, we don't grow out of these as we grow up, but we do develop more creative ways to satisfy the impulses. This **impulse to reach up and cover the mouth** might be masked by someone scratching their nose or turning their head to cough briefly. The impulse is satiated, and our social standing remains intact.

As you've learned thus far, not all these deception behaviors indicate deception in every situation. Sometimes they indicate stress, and other times, we just don't know.

For example, in social situations, covering the mouth is seen as a respectful way to listen to someone. We tend to do this to subconsciously prevent ourselves from interrupting, and it's often a respectful gesture when we speak to others.

In deception, this may be the most reliable indicator of lying. Research suggests that facial touching is the most commonly seen indicator of deception in westernized countries.

In sales or interviewing, it's important to note when you see this behavior. It can indicate respect, concern, uncertainty, and deception.

THE FIG LEAF

This gesture occurs when a **man** folds his hand in front of his genitals. The hands draw inward and rest or cover the crotch area. While we tend to imagine this as a still image with both hands over the crotch area, I'd once more like to suggest you imagine this, and all of these behaviors, as moving images. As practitioners of this art, we are concerned with movement and changes, not still shots.

The term for this behavior was coined by Allan Pease. It tends to indicate that a person is either feeling **vulnerable, threatened, or insecure**.

SCENARIO:

You're seated with someone and going over details of a contract. His hands are gently placed on his legs as he listens. Right when you mention the payment terms, you observe his hands retreating toward his crotch area. As you notice this, you ask a few questions about the terms to determine if there is an issue or if he'd like to modify them, and he opens up. He admits he disagreed with the extended timeline of the contract and would like to change it to reflect payment over a shorter period of time.

You were able to identify the movement as genital-protective behavior and resolve the issue before you got to the point of no return.

SINGLE-ARM WRAP

Remember, while men perform the 'fig leaf,' **women** are likely to perform the single-arm wrap. This behavior indicates the same internal feelings as the fig leaf: feeling **vulnerable, threatened, or insecure**.

Women will instinctively cross an arm across their body and hold the opposite arm, covering the area near their uterus. You can see this behavior in high schools and college campuses anywhere. Where women are in or around new social situations and unknown groups of people, this behavior flourishes.

Much like the fig leaf, the movement is what you are looking for. When one arm begins to fold across the lower abdomen, that's the time to identify the conversational context.

SCENARIO:

As a therapist, you're interviewing a young woman who's complaining of depression. She talks about her family life and childhood, and as she says the word 'stepfather,' she performs a single-arm wrap. You observe the behavior and recognize there may be an issue. During the next therapy session, you ask about this and discover a traumatic history she wouldn't have revealed without your questioning her.

ELBOW-CLOSURE

Fear makes us protect arteries. It's an impressive system we're born with designed to save us from tigers, but it's no longer the threat we face today.

The upper bone in your arm is called the humerus. Elbow closure is when these bones move inward toward the torso. If someone you're speaking to suddenly moves their arms inward, you've established a strong data point worth dealing with. This is mostly visible only when someone is seated.

This fear behavior is also indicative of stress or anxiety. The arms will instinctively pull into the body to protect the brachial artery near the armpit.

SCENARIO:

You are at a party, and you've just met someone. You both sit to chat, and you notice instant elbow closure the moment you mention swimming. Later, you discover she has a fear of water due to a childhood experience. You refer her to a good friend who deals with phobias and save the day.

DOWNWARD PALMS

We show our palms to others to indicate sincerity. Imagine a kid explaining his innocence to his parents. We instantly imagine the arms out to the side, with palms exposed to the parents.

Throughout our lives, we participate in conversations. You've likely seen this behavior tens of thousands of times without noticing it. We expose our palms to indicate sincerity or openness, but they face downward to indicate the opposite.

When someone is seated, their hands will be resting on their legs, the table, or the arms of a chair most of the time. The downward palm behavior occurs when someone's hands turn downward toward the table or body, further concealing the palm from view. This gesture can be subtle, but it's easy to spot after only a few rounds of practice.

This can indicate **disagreement, stress, concealment, deception, or even anger**, depending on the context. If we see this in sales, for instance, we might be seeing an objection to something being discussed. However, in the courtroom we may be seeing a reluctance to proceed with questions or concealment of information.

SCENARIO:

You're at your doctor's office. You talk her through all the symptoms you are having, and she takes notes on a notepad. Before prescribing you anything, she asks what other medications you're currently taking. You let her know you are taking a certain prescription from another doctor, and notice her palms turn down onto her legs as she listens. Later, you ask her if she thinks you should keep taking the prescription from the other doctor, and she convinces you not to do so. She was hesitant to undermine the other doctor, but lets you know that the medication could be more dangerous than you thought with your condition.

SUMMARY

There's no behavior for deception, only stress. So whether or not you're locked in an interrogation room with suspects, the same behaviors will benefit you.

Don't worry, at the end of this book, I'm going to detail out exactly how to learn all of this, and I've even typed up a training planning guide for you that's included here in the book as well.

Coming up, I will actually show you the techniques that FBI spy hunters and intelligence operatives use to get information out of people...without them even knowing.

CHAPTER 8

ELICITATION

These are highly effective skills. People are usually underwhelmed when getting trained to use these skills, as they seem simplistic. The underwhelm quickly vanishes when they apply the techniques in conversation. They are nothing short of astounding.

Elicitation is the art of obtaining information without asking many questions. The techniques you're about to learn are by far the most effective information-gathering tools taught to intelligence agencies and spies all over the world. However, these techniques do more than just make someone divulge information.

When someone discusses sensitive information with you, a bond forms, someone who has already begun sharing secrets is highly likely to continue doing so. Think of the last time you were able to talk without a filter to someone. I am not sure where it is, but there's some kind of switch in our brains that flips when we start talking. This switch makes us more connected with the other person and opens up the gates for even *more* information to come out.

You've probably used a couple of these techniques before without knowing it. And you've heard them from others without realizing it as well. Now you'll be able to use them on purpose instead of by accident. When I teach these to intelligence personnel, they are always completely in shock at how effective they are in such a short time.

With the core of 6MX being reading human behavior, these techniques make it more powerful. If we'd like to read someone, it would really help to make them comfortable revealing more information than they usually do. And all these techniques can be used in under six minutes, adding critical data to your behavior profile of anyone you speak to

HOW ELICITATION WORKS

Elicitation works in three ways:

1. The elicitation techniques are subtle and sound conversational and social
2. The information doesn't feel forced out of them—statements are used instead of questions, making it feel more natural
3. The information flow has a compound effect—as it begins to feel more comfortable, the person becomes more likely to continue to reveal more information

The more sensitive the information you need, the fewer questions you should ask.

Let's imagine you and I are standing in the produce section of a grocery store. A female employee is stocking new oranges into a pile. I give you an assignment: approach this employee and find out how much she earns per hour in less than sixty seconds.

In this scenario, you might initially think of walking up to her and asking her how much money she makes. You might get an answer, but you'll get more than that. In our culture, money and sex are taboo conversational topics. Asking someone about their level of income is offensive, and even if you got the answer you were looking for, you'd still be instantly put into a column in her mind of being anti-social, rude, or just awkward. This is not ideal.

If we ask questions to discover sensitive information, the person might feel as though you're prying. People tend to recoil when they feel interrogated. When they provide the information we need voluntarily, they feel much better about it and will remember the conversation as a good one.

Back to the produce section. What if you watched me obtain the information using elicitation?

I walk up to the employee and ask her where the celery is, and as she's walking me over to that area, I make a brief comment about an article I just read online. "I just read this article on the news that said you guys all got bumped up to 21 dollars an hour a few weeks ago. That's fantastic!" The employee gives me a confused look and says, "*What?* No. We only make 14.75 an hour here unless you're a manager. Managers make like 19.50."

Not only did she voluntarily offer her income, but I even got the exact amount, and the manager's income without using a question to do so!

Elicitation can be used to warm up a quiet client, get your kids to tell you more about their day, or obtain national intelligence-level secrets.

Using the skills effectively requires good listening skills and suppression of the desire to talk about ourselves. In most communication, these are the skills we need anyway.

Good elicitation should sound and feel like a normal conversation. The skills you're about to learn are effective anywhere.

ELICITATION SKILLS: PART ONE

Elicitation is effective for several reasons, but the main reason is that it allows the person to recall actively offering the information instead of being questioned or interrogated.

THE HOURGLASS METHOD

This method is taught in government intelligence training around the world. It relies on two psychological principles that describe how we remember things:

1. **The Primacy Effect**—our tendency to remember the beginning of things such as numbers, conversations, and events with greater clarity than the middle.

2. **The Recency Effect**—our tendency to remember the ending (the most recent happenings) of things such as numbers, conversations, and events with greater clarity than the middle

The hourglass method uses these two principles by ensuring the sensitive information we need is couched within the middle of conversations. If this occurs, the person being elicited is far more likely to remember the beginning and end of the conversation. The memory of giving up information is far more likely to be remembered with less detail.

In a conversation, for example, you might start by discussing topics loosely related to the information you need to gather from someone. After this, you would narrow down the focus to the desired information you're seeking. After eliciting the desired information, you can simply walk the conversation back to general topics about other things.

If I wanted to obtain information from someone about a past relationship, my plan might look like this:

- Discuss relationships in general
- Talk about a past relationship of my own
- Obtain the details of their relationship
- Redirect conversation to dating
- Talk about living in modern times with dating apps

I focused the conversation around **general topics that are close to the sensitive topic** I'd like to obtain information about.

This is in no way a requirement to use elicitation. You can use elicitation in almost any scenario without the Hourglass Method being necessary. The Hourglass Method should only be applied in instances where you need vital, sensitive information. Remember, elicitation is a technique to gather information, but it is far more effective than just an information-gathering tool; it produces an uncommon connection to the other person.

As someone realizes they are sharing more information than they usually do, there's a switch in the brain that flips. This switch activates all kinds of connection, trust, and openness. Elicitation can do this all on its own.

THE HUMAN FACTORS THAT MAKE ELICITATION POSSIBLE

We all have a few human traits that allow elicitation to work. We all share some of them, and others you'll find to be stronger in different people (more on that later).

THE NEED TO BE RECOGNIZED

Our need to feel like we've done a great job or have achieved something is often something we look to others to confirm. This need for recognition shows up in many ways.

DIFFIDENCE

We all tend to downplay compliments when we get them most times. Our responses to compliments and praise will often contain an explanation or admission. Compliments can be viewed as a digging tool. When someone receives a compliment, we typically will get more information from them instead of a 'thank you.'

CORRECTING THE RECORD

When we hear inaccurate information, and we know otherwise, we tend to offer the correct information in response immediately. In the example earlier, with the woman in the produce department in the grocery store, you saw a perfect example of this when we told her incorrect information.

WE WANT TO BE HEARD

We love talking about ourselves. Especially when someone is interested and engaging in conversation. Our stories, successes, skills, and desires are very important to us, and we tend to enjoy sharing these things with others. When someone is interested in our story, we share.

WE WANT TO OFFER ADVICE

When someone is particularly interested, we open up. But when they begin to ask for advice about things we're knowledgeable about, we really open up! Our tendency to become excited and open when someone expresses a degree of naïveté about the subject of our expertise is hardwired.

WE WILL OFFER INFORMATION TO THOSE THAT DISAGREE

When someone disagrees or doesn't believe us, we will go to great lengths to make it right. We will offer up all kinds of information in defense of what we know or how we feel. Our knowledge and beliefs are two things we will defend with all we got—and all we got in most conversations is information. This trigger works exceedingly well when meeting new people, as you'll see in the next section.

ELICITATION SKILLS: PART TWO

FOR CONVERSATIONS

Let's go over a few techniques you can use in just about every conversation you have. These techniques are fantastic for getting the information you want, but they are even better at creating connections with others.

While the techniques that follow will seem like individual blocks that can snap together, they are much more fluid—they can be woven together to form longer statements or be used individually.

PROVOCATIVE STATEMENTS

A provocative statement is any statement that **provokes a response**. For instance, if someone told you they worked in a medical facility, your response may be something like, "Wow. I bet that's an interesting job."

No doubt, you would get a response from them, and maybe even a descriptive story about how 'interesting' their job really is. Mission complete!

Provocative statements can take many forms. Any statement you make in response to someone's words can serve as a provocative statement.

EXAMPLE 1:

> **Client:** "I've been traveling most of the month."
>
> **You:** "You've got to be exhausted."
>
> **Client:** "You wouldn't believe it; three of my flights got delayed, and I was stuck in airports for almost a forty-eight-hour period. I had to miss Danielle's birthday, and we missed a major contract with a pharmaceutical company in Boston because of it."

In this example, the simple statement you made caused an outpouring of information. The client has given you a lot of information. All you did here was make a short, concise statement.

EXAMPLE 2:

> **Person:** "I've been watching the kids all week. It's been hard to reach out."
>
> **You:** "Sounds like a tough week for sure."
>
> **Person:** "I don't know what to do now. I got buried in email. Susan is supposed to be coming back on Friday, though."

EXAMPLE 3:

> **You:** "I bet this is a great place to work!"
>
> **Cashier:** "It's not that bad. We get pretty good hours."
>
> **You:** "I imagine you guys have to keep busy with all the storms coming in."
>
> **Cashier:** "It's been insane recently; we've had to take extra shifts to fill the back of the store with stuff we probably won't sell. They like to stock us

up for the smallest storms, and we don't have room in the back for all the food. Most of it ends up being thrown out. It's sad."

In this example, we stacked two provocative statements together to gain even more information.

EXAMPLE 4:

> **Call center employee:** "I can see your account, and I've made the changes you requested."
> **You:** "Thanks so much. You guys must be on the phones all day."
> **Call center employee:** "Yes. It's pretty busy here. We work nine-hour shifts most of the time."
> **You:** "Nine hours...that's a long time!"
> **Call center employee:** "We get to pick our days, though. Most of the time, the phones are ringing non-stop. People call in a lot. Next time you call, you can press *22 and go straight to the front of the line if you like."
> **You:** "Thanks!"

In this example, the small connection you formed by getting them to talk paid off! As you move through the next technique, try to imagine how you can apply this in conversations to make it something you do automatically.

INFORMATIONAL ALTRUISM

We have a human tendency to feel compelled to do something for someone if they do something for us. When someone shares something sensitive with us, it's a little bit awkward if we don't reciprocate with something similar.

If you're in a conversation, and you share a personal problem you're having with someone, the other person starts to feel an obligation to do the same.

Suppose you wanted to get sensitive business information from someone. In that case, you'd need to use the Hourglass Method and discuss business and the company, in general, before using this technique, but the rest of the conversation might sound like this:

You: "...I just don't get it. Our security staff are falling way behind. We have these barcode scanners for our employee ID cards that are supposed to unlock the main door to let you into the building, but I scanned a barcode on a candy bar a few weeks ago, and it let me in. People have even gotten in scanning their gym membership cards."

Person: "Oh, man. That's bad. We have a similar issue, our employee ID cards are yellow, and the security staff are so far away from the entrance that you could just wrap a Post-It note around your driver's license, and they will buzz you right into the door."

The person you're speaking with feels almost **compelled to tell a similar story** or share something similar to what you've shared.

If you wanted to gain information about someone's ex-partner, you might begin by talking about relationships and transition to a discussion about your ex-partner first, revealing personal information in the process. They would feel compelled to do the same.

In a sense, you're not only giving them information so they feel compelled to share similar things, but you're also giving the information out to permit them to be equally open in the conversation.

This technique also works in reverse. If someone tells you something particularly sensitive or private, you can do the same in order to make them feel as thorough there is a mutual exchange of information taking place.

FLATTERY

We all like flattery, but that's not the purpose of this technique. Flattery and compliments tend to activate our innate desire to appear humble. In our efforts to appear modest, we tend to spill more information than we otherwise would.

When someone dismisses a compliment or explains away something with self-effacement, they will **reveal a deeper level of information** with each flattery/compliment statement we make.

EXAMPLE 1:

>**You:** "That was a great job. It was easy to tell who led this whole thing."
>
>**Them:** "Well, thanks, but it wasn't all me. We had a good team."
>
>**You:** "No doubt, but I'm sure they realized who really brought it all together."
>
>**Them:** "They were the ones who did most of the work. We had a lot of setbacks, too, that most

people don't even see or hear about. We had to hire outside help from another state just to get it all done on time."

As they continue to provide explanations in order to dismiss the compliment, more information flows.

While offering compliments is a great way to get information, it's not recommended that you use this more than a few times, as it's not socially-smart or even good conversation.

EXAMPLE 2:

You: "This is the cleanest Uber I've ever ridden in!"

Driver: "Thanks. I try to keep it clean, but it's hard with the hours I keep."

You: "I can imagine. But it looks really amazing."

Driver: "I try to keep it clean. I'm usually working nights and picking up drunk morons who occasionally vomit in here. I go to the local hospitals a lot too for pickups."

You: *Sanitizes hands after exiting.

ELICITING COMPLAINTS

Most of us don't complain to strangers. But when we do, it's freeing. We get to vent to someone and often don't realize how much information we are providing them.

When we use elicitation to get someone to complain, we can also identify their negative GHT (Gestural Hemispheric Tendency) side. This outpouring of information also serves to create a connection, as the person sees genuine empathy and is able to speak to you in **ways they don't typically speak to others**.

Let's examine how we can use the other techniques of elicitation to elicit complaints from someone.

If we went with a provocative statement, we could simply comment on the negative aspects of something they might be likely to complain about. If you were in an Uber and made a comment such as, "I bet you guys don't get much of the money paid through the app," you're very likely going to get lots of information about their income and complaints about the company in general.

If we decided to use the Citations Method, we could comment that we heard something from a friend or read something negative in an article. We could even say we read something very positive in order to have them correct us, triggering the need to correct the record.

EXAMPLE 1: (Using Provocative Statements)

> **You:** "I bet the hours here are difficult to work with."
>
> **Person:** "It's been tough. We get assigned all kinds of shifts, but they are never the same, so I have to rearrange daycare at the beginning of every week when the schedule comes out."
>
> **You:** "Yikes. I had no idea they did all that to you guys."
>
> **Person:** "That's not even the half of it..."

Using a simple, provocative statement, you were able to get them to open more than they ever have to a customer. With one more provocative statement as a follow-up, you opened the gates even wider.

EXAMPLE 2: (Using Citations)

> **You:** "I just read online that people have been leaving the company a lot."
>
> **Employee:** "Yeah, I think the management has made some bad decisions with staffing. Our hotel doesn't even have a manager right now."
>
> **You:** "Wow. I had no idea. The article said most of the employees who left went to another hotel chain."
>
> **Employee:** "I don't doubt it. They probably went to Marriott. They are well-known for treating their people well. It's not that bad, but there's not much we can do if we work the front desk. Would you like an upgrade?""

Using two similar Citation techniques, we were able to develop a much faster bond; as the person complained a bit, they felt like they were able to voice their opinion. Since you were there to hear it, it feels like a good connection that developed organically.

CITATIONS

When we went through the example of the grocery store employee and obtaining her income, this is what was used.

When we cite or reference something we saw, heard, or read about, we are using citations. This helps to elicit information because it **allows someone to fulfill the desire to correct the record** or offer additional information.

If you're speaking to someone who works in a bank, and you'd like to figure out when a new branch is opening, you should use Citations. You might simply tell them you read somewhere online that they will be opening the bank's new branch in November. In reply, they're likely to correct you. You might get a response such as, "Oh! Actually, it's going to be a lot sooner. It's set to open in June as of now."

EXAMPLE 1:

- You'd like to start a conversation with an A/C repair person about how much they charge compared to other companies.

You: "I was just looking online last night, and I saw this article that said so many repair companies compete on pricing, and a lot of them have lower prices for smaller jobs to build relationships with homeowners."

In response, you will probably hear a lot about their opinions on that, and they will most likely discuss the pricing in their own company.

EXAMPLE 2:

- You are in sales and looking to establish how much your competition offered to perform services to your client.

You: "I've just heard from a few folks that they got offered a gig to work with them for about 13,000."

If the information is inaccurate, the client will most likely correct the record and set you straight. If it's accurate, they will confirm it and offer even more information about the offer.

EXAMPLE 3:

- You're on a first date, and you'd like to find out how often the other person does this kind of thing. You'll want to offer up a huge number in order for them to appear much 'better' than the people who go on first dates all the time.

You: "It's crazy. I just read something recently that said most men in the US go on an average of twelve first dates before they find someone they are happy with."

In their response, they will likely spill their own habits. Instead of twelve, they might admit to their own dating experiences and how often they go on first dates.

VERBAL REFLECTION

When someone mentions what they do, where they work, where they live, or almost anything else, we have an opportunity to reflect a bit of understanding and connection.

When we hear our words and ideas reflected by someone we are speaking to, a connection forms, and we get more information.

There are two main methods for this. The first is the Verbal Mirror technique taught by the FBI. In this technique, when someone speaks, the final few words (usually the final three), are the most important. When they finish a statement or question, repeat the final three words.

EXAMPLE 1:

> **Prospect:** "I really think we could do this deal if I were able to get the full package."
> **You:** "The full package?"
> **Prospect:** "Yes. I mean the order, deliveries, and the follow up all in one custom offer."
> **You:** "Easy. We can do that in one custom offer."

We obtained more information and a crystal-clear picture of what the client was actually looking for. It flowed more easily from their lips because they weren't being asked specific questions, and they were able to clarify exactly what they needed to make the deal happen.

EXAMPLE 2: (Police Officer)

> **Suspect:** "I tried to get them to stop, but they kept telling me no."
> **You:** "Telling you no?"
> **Suspect:** "Yes. They continued to throw everything out the window to get rid of it. Johnny still has a lot of the drugs in his house, though."
> **You:** "In his house?"
> **Suspect:** "Yep. He keeps it all inside cereal boxes in his pantry."

Simple repetition made more information flow out of the suspect in this example. The final few words are often the most important when someone is speaking. All we need to do is say them back. Whether it's in statement-form or question-form doesn't matter. If you go back to those examples, you could change all of the question marks to periods, and it would still cause a very similar verbal reaction from the person across the table.

The second way you can perform this is to repeat the *general theme* of what you've heard instead of specific words. I've seen the best results from my trainees when they use Theme Repetition, followed by a provocative statement. To do this, simply reflect back to the theme of what was just said, followed right away by a provocative statement.

EXAMPLE 3: (On a plane)

> **Guy:** "I've been an orthopedic surgeon for almost eleven years now."
>
> **You:** "Saving lives. I bet it's a really rewarding job."

In this example you reflected a general theme back to the person and used a provocative statement to elicit further information. You would have likely gotten a lot more information and possibly complaints from the doctor seated beside you.

EXAMPLE 4: (Dating)

> **Woman:** "There are so many reasons I love keeping bees. They are the best employees I've ever had."
>
> **You:** "Beekeeping. I bet that took a long time to learn."

In the simplest form, you reflected back the theme of her statement in a single word and followed it with a provocative statement.

EXAMPLE 5: (Sales)

> **Client:** "I've been working in the oil industry for fifteen years. I've seen a whole lot."
>
> **You:** "Long time. I can only imagine all the deals you've made."

As the man put the emphasis on fifteen years, you noticed that was the important part of his statement. You repeated the theme of that back with two words. Those two words would usually suffice to draw more information out, but the provocative statement ensures it.

This technique is nothing short of magic. It works in almost unlimited situations and creates a massive opening for the person to speak and offer up more information. There is one drawback, however. Using it too much can cause the conversation to be awkward. Let them be a part of the elicitation toolkit as a whole, instead of a single go-to technique.

NAÏVETÉ

When we are proud of something and meet someone interested in it, it's hard to resist the urge to educate them a bit. When using naïveté, we have to consider three factors:

1. We need to express ignorance about the topic
2. We need to express interest or fascination with the topic

3. The topic needs to be something they take pride in knowing, such as a skill, trade, educational background, or expertise.

The **urge to educate others** lies within all of us. When you apply these three principles, the elicitation will be much stronger, and the flow of information is virtually limitless.

EXAMPLE 1: (Airplane)

> **Person:** "I actually wrote my thesis on the fish population; how they are dwindling over time."
>
> **You:** "That's absolutely fascinating. I have always been really interested in learning about that. Granted, I literally know next to nothing about it."

EXAMPLE 2: (Business)

> **Employee:** "I've been working around the clock on this Excel spreadsheet. I think the formulas I put into the financial columns are going to blow your mind."
>
> **You:** "That's awesome. Thanks. I've always wanted to know how all of that stuff works. It's fascinating. I can barely copy and paste into those things."

EXAMPLE 3: (New client)

> **Client:** "...Yeah, I've been a videographer for most of my life now. I've got several films under my belt."
>
> **You:** "How incredible! I have always wanted to know how that all works. It's so interesting to me. I can barely make a movie on my phone!"

CRITICISM

This one is tough. When criticized, the person you're speaking to may feel compelled to provide information in defense of the situation.

Criticism isn't usually directly about the person; it can be about a topic around the current situation, the company they work for, or even someone they know. When you offer criticism, it should be indirect. The criticism is only designed to make someone **feel the need to justify or clarify something** by providing you with information.

EXAMPLE 1: (Dating)

> **You:** "It's really a shame so many people don't open up and just be themselves."

Using this technique, they will not only agree with you, but also give you information on their thoughts. As a second bonus, they will also make a silent, unconscious agreement to be more open during the conversation.

EXAMPLE 2: (Buying a car)

> **You:** "I hear so many people tell me that these cars don't last that long."
>
> **Salesman:** "Wow. I don't hear that often. They actually have a wonderful track record. I will admit that last year, there were a lot of recalls, and they took a hit in the market for it. But this year's model is upgraded from that, and our service department has parts on hand for any anticipated recalls that might be coming this year."

You: "Well. That's good, but the expected issues this year are all different from what I've heard. They aren't the same issues."

Salesman: "True. But the steering wheel thing isn't major, and the airbag deployment issue is expected to be resolved within the next few months."

By simply using two complaints, you were able to uncover quite a bit of valuable information.

Sometimes, in order to soften the severity of the complaint, you can reference someone else. Instead of the criticism coming from you, you can remove it to a third party. In the example above, we cited an article in order for the complaint to be more casually mentioned and indirect.

You can also use the 'someone told me' or 'I heard from a friend that...' to soften complaints.

When offering complaints, keep rapport and trust as the key point of focus.

BRACKETING

A range is sometimes better than single digits. When you need numbers, such as dates, times, ages, etc., you can give a range and let someone 'correct the record.' Instead of saying a single number to trigger the need to correct the record, sometimes a range of numbers will do.

Let's step back to the produce-woman example and examine how that would sound:

You: "I just read an article that all the employees here got bumped up to somewhere between 21 and 29 dollars per hour. That's fantastic!"

The range of numbers might be **more likely to trigger a response** from someone.

EXAMPLE 1: (Business)

>**You:** "I heard you guys were going to be doing like 12-17 deals this month."
>
>**Them:** "Actually, it's going to be more like 8 or 9."

EXAMPLE 2: (Business)

>**You:** "I read somewhere that the company is going to be moving operations out of California next summer."
>
>**Them:** "Not next summer. It's going to be a lot sooner than that for sure. Probably February."

EXAMPLE 3: (Police)

>**You:** "So, we're mostly hearing there was about 10 to 14 grams of the substance in the car."
>
>**Suspect:** "What? No! It was only like a gram at best!"

EXAMPLE 4: (Buying a car)

>**You:** "I've read so many things saying you guys get between 3,000 to 5,000 over invoice on your vehicles."
>
>**Saleswoman:** "Actually, it's a lot closer to 1,200."

When we provide a range, people can be more likely to give us an accurate number. The range of numbers we offer up is undefined and non-distinct, making the other person more likely to want to provide you with something more concrete.

DISBELIEF

This might be one of the most powerful elicitation techniques out there. When we express disbelief in response to something, people will typically offer even more information to help us understand or to convince us.

The Disbelief technique works because, as humans, we tend to want to be believed. When someone expresses any kind of doubt, we feel **compelled to open the floodgates of information** so that we can set the record straight, convince someone it's as bad as we say it is, or explain in more detail.

EXAMPLE 1: (Sales)

> **You:** "There's no way you guys are making a profit with just online sales. It's so hard with the economy right now."
>
> **Client:** "We're doing really well. Sales have even spiked this year."
>
> **You:** "That sounds amazing, but everyone is struggling; you guys had to take some losses."
>
> **Client:** "Actually, we are hiring new people. We just wrapped this quarter with three million in gross."

The client offered more information either because they thought you didn't believe it, or you didn't have enough data to form a belief in the first place. Either way, you elicited a lot of valuable information.

EXAMPLE 2: (Airplane)

>**Person:** "Yeah, it was bad. They fired him."
>
>**You:** "What? I've seen him on television; he seems like the nicest person in the world. There's no way that many people would dislike him."
>
>**Person:** "It's worse than you think. He's a totally different person when there aren't cameras around. He was an asshole."
>
>**You:** "There's no way I would believe he's rude to people. He seems so nice."
>
>**Person:** "You have no idea. He even punched an intern in the face once. Got swept under the rug, 'cause they didn't want a legal battle. They are holding that against him if he goes public against the company.

Stacking disbelief works to uncover more information. And you've probably noticed that there are provocative statements woven into many of these techniques here. Those add power to the disbelief method, making the person more likely to respond to the disbelief *and* the statement, giving you even more information.

SUMMARY

With what seems like a simple method, you'd be absolutely amazed at the results you can get from people using these. They don't have to be used in order, and they can be applied anywhere. In less than a nine-minute drive using a rideshare app, I showed one of my clients that I was able to use all of these techniques in a short period of time. The information that came forth from our driver was remarkable, extremely personal, and even contained information about the company we probably shouldn't be hearing about.

In the next chapter, we'll take a close look at how to surgically analyze hidden information in language that exposes hidden fears, drives, and even the exact words someone needs to hear to make decisions.

KNOWLEDGE CHECK

1. How would you trigger a need to correct the record?

2. What technique would be best to get someone to talk about their company's revenue?

3. How would you use disbelief to make a police officer tell you more about the things she's seen on the job?

CHAPTER 9

THE HUMAN NEEDS MAP

We all need stuff.

Abraham Maslow even made a pyramid for it. The Maslow Hierarchy of Needs illustrates what us human need to live and be happy.

Maslow broke down human needs into 6 categories:

1. **Physiological Needs**—food, water, health, sleep, clothing, shelter
2. **Safety Needs**—security from predators, financial security, well-being, medicine
3. **Social Belonging**—friendship, social groups, intimacy, family or tribe
4. **Self-Esteem**—confidence, competence, independence, freedom
5. **Self-Actualization**—spouse or partner, parenting, self-development, goal-pursuits
6. **Transcendence** (added to the hierarchy much later)—a desire to leave an impact, legacy, spirituality, altruism

In a business sense, the higher-level needs have a much more powerful influence over our behavior than those toward the bottom of the list. Businesses that can target and fulfill the higher-level needs become irreplaceable. Once the base needs are met, the customer will continue to strive for the next need. This is how customer loyalty is created.

In the 6MX process, the social and physical needs don't play a major role in most of our conversations, and we need to look for other indicators that provide real-time results when we identify them.

The Human Needs Map does just that.

While it likely won't stand up to academic scrutiny, I believe there is a vast difference between academic-based and results-based skills. The needs map you're going to learn here is the result of twenty years of research and instruction in teaching elite groups of influencers how to speed-read people they communicate with.

The Human Needs Map© is a tool to identify someone's social needs , not just what they need physically. So many of our decisions are made within the mammalian brain that the social needs drive more of our behavior than we know.

If you're able to identify someone's social needs, you have access to far more information than you might imagine. The social needs—what we need from other people—reveal the drives of our behavior and even some of our most secret fears. In almost any conversation, you should be able to identify social needs within the first two minutes. Six minutes is a worst-case-scenario. People reveal so much about themselves in the first few minutes of conversation that I think you may be shocked.

Download a high-resolution Needs Map at
www.chasehughes.com/6mxbookresources

There are six needs on the Needs Map: three primary drives and three secondary drives. Almost anyone you speak to will have one primary need and one secondary need. Keep in mind none of these needs indicate anything bad about anyone. We are all equally 'messed up' in our own way.

The primary Needs:
Significance, Approval, and Acceptance

The secondary Needs:
Intelligence, Pity, and Strength

THE PRIMARY SOCIAL NEEDS

The three primary needs are significance, approval, and acceptance. Each of these represents a question the person is asking, their hidden fears, and behavioral indicators of each need.

We will dissect each of the needs using four steps:
1. What is the definition of this need?
2. What is the question they are asking internally in social situations?
3. What are the behavioral indicators of this need?
4. What are the visible indicators I can see to identify it?

SIGNIFICANCE

Definition:
This need is a desire to **feel** significant and is confirmed by the behaviors of others around them.

Question:
The significance-driven person is internally asking, 'Do others view me as significant and making an impact?'

Behavioral Indicators:
The need for significance shows itself in people who behave in ways that tend to make the most impact on those around them. They will typically speak about their accomplishments, impact on their community, and the way they have contributed to their workplace or family. They will be drawn toward projects, activities, and tasks that make them stand out from the crowd, become more memorable, or create a way for them to deviate from the norm to be seen as an outlier.

Outward Indicators:
- Designed to stand out
- Obvious wealth indicators
- Contributions to a cause on bumper stickers, shirts, or bags
- Openly conveying wealth
- Novel and distinctive facial hair
- Showing musculature
- Clothing showing musculature
- Showing cleavage

- Focus conversations on themselves
- Status symbols—watches, cars, clothing, brands
- Want to be first to make decisions in a group—leading the charge
- Latest model of mobile phone or computers

The significance need is relatively easy to spot in almost any conversation. Later, we will go through a few examples to illustrate how easy they are to spot.

APPROVAL / RECOGNITION

Definition:

The approval-needs people we speak to are looking for **permission and recognition**. They will typically make comments that are self-deprecating in order for you to offer approval in return. You might hear something like, 'I don't know if I can do the presentation today; I suck at public speaking.' They say this in order to hear something along the lines of, 'No, you don't! You did a great job last time, and you need to stop doubting yourself!'

We've all met these people, and we all know a few of them at work or within our family. We will get into how these play into persuasive communication in a bit

Question:

'Do others provide me with recognition, allowing me to move forward with confidence?'

Behavioral Indicators:

Will perform several acts in order to seek approval from others. They will change their position in order to gain approval when someone disapproves of their views. Will typically ask permission to do things when it isn't needed. Will often coerce people into giving them compliments in order to feel good.

Outward Indicators:

- Rigidness
- Commonly feel impostor syndrome
- Derive strength from professional success
- More formally dressed or a notch above the rest of the crowd
- Standing out to compensate for impostor syndrome
- Frequent competition participation, regardless of the type
- More inclined to seek singular romantic partners
- Will carry medicine or things to give to others
- Will eat or drink beverages they don't like
- Less likely to complain to employees of restaurants
- Less likely to send food back
- Less likely to argue or request refunds
- • Overtly pays compliments
- Will be self-deprecating in order to hear someone tell them they are wrong

ACCEPTANCE

Definition:
The acceptance-needs people we speak to are concerned with **membership**, groups, tribes, teams, and connections. These are the people who get tattoos that show membership in groups, they will have bumper stickers that show they belong to organizations and will talk about things that indicate the associations they are a member of.

Question:
'Do I belong, and do others see that I do?'

Behavioral Indicators:
These subjects will exhibit behaviors that draw appreciation and benefit others. They are interested in actively contributing to the well-being of those around them. Will show need for social acceptance through conformity (even if it is feigned). These subjects will be drawn to activities that help others, such as volunteering, cooking, helping animals, and participating in protests for things they believe in.

Outward Indicators:
- Prone to membership of all types
- Easily swayed—ideal cult members
- Biker gangs, fitness groups, fitness teams
- Attracted to careers that help others, like cooking, healthcare, and therapy
- More likely to have multiple pets
- Will change appearance to suit (please) the environment they are in

- Less likely to have eccentric or unique identity formed and developed
- Smaller dogs as common pets
- Strong sense of community
- Wears shirts that indicate membership, tribes
- Returns all eyebrow flashes
- More likely to do favors for others
- Will move out of the way as others approach on the street

SECONDARY SOCIAL NEEDS

INTELLIGENCE

Definition:
The intelligence-needs people will discuss things that allow you to **notice how educated or intelligent they are**. From what they wrote their thesis on in college to large dictionary words and phrases to show their intellectual prowess, you'll hear information that regularly draws your attention back to their intelligence and smarts.

Question:
'Do others view me as smart or intelligent?'

Behavioral Indicators:
These subjects have a need to be seen as intelligent and will exhibit behaviors that allude to their intellectual prowess or education. They will speak about their education, expertise, and how they have assisted others in their endeavors using

their intellect. Tying their need to feel intelligent to your goal helps them to align their needs with yours automatically. Ensure compliance by acknowledging their need for power – make them feel like they're the one in charge initially or compliment their leadership.

Outward Indicators:
- Break patterns and norms
- More likely to be sexually deviant (legally)
- Less effort into appearance than others
- Bowties
- Shirts advertising their university
- College rings after the age of 25
- Deliberately enhanced vernacular
- Asking if you know things they know you don't
- Over-emphasizes the intellectual aspect of stories

PITY

Definition:
We all know a few of these people. They will complain about stuff all the time, from traffic jams and weather, to 'that thing' that happened to them a long time ago. Keep in mind that they are **asking you to confirm that they have it bad** or that they are in unique circumstances not many others are facing.

Question:
'Do others realize and recognize how bad I've had it?'

Behavioral Indicators:
Pity subjects seek pity, sympathy, or co-misery. They will discuss pitfalls, tragedy, misfortune, and annoyances to gain sympathy or support from others. They will express this through stories or conversations wherein they complain about being victimized or having 'bad luck.' Confirming the severity of their condition is the fastest way to build rapport. It's best to follow their complaints with a brief pause before responding, so they feel understood and fully 'heard.'

Outward Indicators:
- Typically unhealthy appearance
- Hunched posture
- Visible disapproval on the face
- Prone to bad health
- Attraction of abusive partners—stay with them longer
- Frequently stressed appearance
- Visible reaction to the tiniest pain
- Broken heart tattoos
- Lots of tattoos (I have a story to tell)
- Medical or non-medical marijuana (shirts, talking about it, leaf shape on bags, etc.)

STRENGTH/ POWER

Definition:

The Strength/Power needs people have a dichotomy: There are highs and lows. On the high-end, we are likely to see people who strive to lead companies, teams, and processes. Their social choices are governed by a **need to be seen as a good leader** or a powerful CEO. They find themselves in these positions not because they are the best fit (most of the time), but because they have spent a long time behaving in ways to be seen as a leader by others. On the low-end, you'll see the person who may have been bullied. They will over-posture, speak louder than necessary, and take actions to remind people that others have less power than they do.

Question:

'Do others see me as powerful and strong?' / 'Do others think I **make a difference?**'

Behavioral Indicators:

Strength and power-needs subjects don't need power. They need to FEEL powerful. This need is primarily fear-based. Strength-needs subjects will display their power in various ways in conversation and in their lives. From stories about toughness under fire to speaking about their individual power over their environment, they are trying to communicate their strength so that they can be SEEN as powerful. This is the 'tough guy,' the 'badass,' and the 'rebel.'

Outward Indicators:

- Obvious display of musculature through clothing
- Deliberate loudness or volume
- Exaggerated posture
- Exaggerated arm movement
- Fight brands like Tap Out, etc.
- Large dogs—aggressive breeds
- Avoids most eye contact during regular activities
- Makes more aggressive eye contact if challenged or threatened
- Aggressive behaviors such as over-posturing and rudeness to store employees
- Heavy metal or death metal listening
- Creates chances to talk about overcoming challenges
- Discusses how they got one over on big companies or high-level people
- Overly concerned with status and social pecking orders

IDENTIFYING HUMAN NEEDS IN CONVERSATION

You will be surprised when you hear how often you've missed key insights into someone's psychology. If this were the only technique you took from the book; your life would still drastically change. When we know what internal questions someone is consistently asking when they interact with people, our language can adapt to what they need to feel and hear.

Within the first few minutes of conversation, especially now that you know exactly how to elicit information, you'll hear people expose their deepest internal drives to you without even knowing it. Let's examine a few phrases and see if you can identify the needs being exposed in each of them.

"I mean, it's no big deal, it was only 80,000 dollars…": *Significance*

"I can't believe I've been sick for an entire week…": *Pity*

"I remember back at Harvard, we had this…": *Intelligence*

"I've been working in this industry for over two decades…": *Significance*

"My friends keep blowing up my phone, non-stop.": *Acceptance*

"We did a lot of work with them in that organization.": *Acceptance*

"I told my wife to shut up until we got off the highway.": *Strength/Power*

"Those microchips are pretty simple, really, not a big deal.": *Intelligence*

"Here's the main reason I'm the go-to resource for those people...": *Intelligence / Significance*

"There's no reason we can't work together; our team would be a great fit.": *Acceptance*

"I can't believe this traffic. It's ridiculous.": *Pity*

"How the hell can these idiots be in charge?": *Intelligence* (use of the word idiots as a derogatory remark about others)

"I really suck at getting these kinds of projects put together.": *Approval*

"I don't know if I'll be able to get it all done; I'm overwhelmed.": *Pity/approval*

"I've actually read a lot of books on that. What you need to do is...": *Intelligence*

"I'm getting so fat these days.": *Approval*

"Everyone here has to go through me in order to approve anything.": *Significance*

"I've only got three days to get this done, and it's a week-long project.": *Pity*

"I typically don't wear those off-brand clothes.": *Significance*

"I can't make it; I actually have a motorcycle rally in Orlando that weekend.": *Acceptance*

"I'm a cancer researcher, but it's gotten so boring. Same thing every day.": *Intelligence*

"Well, I'm a full-time bartender, but I have a YouTube channel with 3 million subscribers.": *Significance*

These are all things we would hear in conversations on a daily basis. It's amazing when I teach this to people to see their reactions, discovering how much they have been missing. But this is only the beginning. You're about to discover something incredible: once you can identify someone's needs, everything changes—you'll reveal a lot more about them than you ever thought possible.

REVEALING HIDDEN FEARS

We are all on the needs map somewhere. Sometimes, in different conversations, we may express conflicting needs. You've no doubt met the badass CEO who you just know turns into a helpless baby when he gets a fever around his wife. At work, he's Significance, at home, he's Pity.

When you identify needs in a conversation, you've identified precisely what they need in this social interaction. This is also the largest, and most effective, **lever you can pull to persuade and influence** their decisions. You know more about their decision processes than most of their close friends and family now.

Since needs are so tied into social behavior, and social behavior is tied directly into our core sense of survival, these needs are pretty strong forces that are at work in the background every day. Each of them carries hidden fear—rooted in tens of millions of years of evolution.

Let's examine the list of needs and expose what fears these people secretly (and likely unconsciously) harbor that drives their behavior. Keep in mind; these fears aren't a word-for-word script but more of a theme that governs them socially.

- **Significance** - abandonment, social ridicule, being ignored, feeling small
- **Approval** - dismissal, disapproval, contempt, feeling left out
- **Acceptance** - social criticism, gossip, peer mismatch
- **Intelligence** - being seen as dumb, being questioned, being 'called out'
- **Pity** - being disregarded, ignored, misunderstood, being disbelieved
- **Strength** - being "punked," disrespected, unacknowledged, challenged

Don't let the size of the list above fool you. Whether you're in a sales office, a courtroom, or an interrogation room, the list above illustrates the precise reasons you will fail to get compliance or the reason the person will choose to comply.

There is no such thing as B2B sales, interrogation, or persuasion in the courtroom; they are all H2H scenarios—human-to-human. It's a social situation between humans that relies heavily on communication, observation, and influence.

EXAMPLE:
You're an attorney involved in a high-stakes case. You've profiled the opposing counsel's client and identified them as a Significance and Intelligence need. You immediately know their fears on the stand revolve around social ridicule and being questioned or challenged. As you stand to cross-examine the opposing counsel's client, your questions are sharper than ever and designed to surgically create emotional reactions. You know exactly how to ask the questions in a way that reflects the person's needs.

EXAMPLE:
You're closing a high-level sales deal worth 3.8 million dollars. You've identified your client as Acceptance and Strength on the Needs Map. Within minutes, you're able to understand that the reasons they want to buy are related to family, friends, and how the purchase will make them seem like a badass to others. You also know the fears of buying will revolve around people talking negatively about him behind his back, social criticism, and being disrespected. Those are the key reasons he may choose not to buy. You're able to highlight the deal in a way to reflect the positive aspects of his needs and avoid the unconscious fears he's wrestling with.

This is one of the most powerful tools I've created in my life, and I intended to keep it as a government-only tool for interrogations. If you harness this power and get comfortable with identifying needs quickly in conversations, you've achieved a level of behavioral skill that not even 99% of psychologists even get training for.

These fears are a lot like little programs that run in the background of your computer. The only difference is that it's next to impossible to open your brain's 'admin settings' and turn them off or delete them. They are so rooted in our biology that they are as forceful as our drive to procreate, except they run in the background, governing our decisions.

WHAT THE NEEDS ACTUALLY MEAN - THE SCARY PART

The Human Needs Map is more than it seems. I'd like to convince you of that now. You've already witnessed how powerful it is at identifying fear and insecurity. But it still carries a power you may not have realized. Let's talk about chemicals.

NEUROPEPTIDES

Neuropeptides are made inside the brain. They are short sequences of amino acids that are co-expressed with neurotransmitters. Essentially, they look like a little twisted paper clip—made out of protein.

They play a major role in behavior, addiction, and habits. When released from the nervous system, these little guys, flood through the body and attach to cells. Our cells have little 'receptor sites' on them that I like to envision looking like a docking station on a spaceship.

The receptors can only receive a specific neuropeptide, however. If a different neuropeptide tries to dock into a receptor site that isn't designed for it, it just won't fit.

Let's pretend, just for a moment, that each of the human needs above are associated with a particular neuropeptide. In the beginning, the surface of our cells have receptor sites on them that can receive all the needs: strength, intelligence, significance, pity, etc.

If a Strength neuropeptide tries to dock into a pity receptor site, no luck.

If someone is a Pity need, they will seek situations and interactions that flood them with specific Pity neuropeptide chemicals. Those little proteins will go to the cells and dock into all of the Pity receptors.

However, over time, the person continues only seek out the 'Pity' neuropeptides. So, all the receptors for the other needs get almost no attention. What ends up happening is that they see the Pity receptors getting all the attention and decide to rebuild themselves into a Pity receptor so they can get in on all the action.

Receptor sites will rebuild themselves in order to receive what the person is always seeking out.

This means, over time, the cells adapt to this person's behavior, and cells become more and more covered with these Pity receptors.

For a moment, let's pause and think about the process of drug-addiction. The same thing happens. As the cells become dependent on a specific chemical, they get upset when it's not coming in. The receptor sites are multiplying, increasing the need for the chemical to be released—more and more often.

The human needs operate in the same way. They become a chemical addiction. When the body isn't getting them, the cells scream at the brain, "Make something happen to get these chemicals!"

The person who is a Pity need may go a day or two without these chemicals. His body begins to scream at him, begging him to get the chemicals. Since these are social needs, he's got to find someone to confirm his pity. When he takes a break from his desk, walks to the break room, and complains about something to a coworker, he's met with a full-body release of chemicals.

In order for him to get the chemicals his body is demanding of him, he has to manufacture a scenario where someone confirms how bad he's had it. The complaints get better and better over time, and he discovers new ways to get the chemicals through tragedy, complaints, being victimized, etc.

This brings us to our secret fifth law of human behavior: **Everyone is a drug addict**. We all just have different drugs.

Our job is to discover these needs, as it shows us what will cause a chemical response.

Now that we're able to identify the needs, we know what will cause a flood of hundreds of millions of neuropeptides to come to life.

We tend to want to tell people they shouldn't feel bad if they complain; if someone is over posturing and obnoxious, we'd like to put them in their place.

Imagine your response to someone in your office complaining about something petty. Your initial desire may be to tell them to 'shut up,' or remind them of all the things they have to be grateful for. **But none of these responses**

**create comfort, openness, or connection with them.
The chemicals do.**

EXAMPLE:

You've been tasked with interrogating a man for aggravated
assault. After hearing this, and a cursory glance through his
social media activity, you determine he is a Strength need
individual. Other interrogators like to go into the room and
remind the suspect who's in charge, but you know better.
Doing that would cause an immediate wall to be built
between the two of you. Instead, you opt for going into the
interrogation room with a calm demeanor, making him feel
like he's more powerful initially. He relaxes as he thinks he's
in charge, and you're able to get a confession within
minutes. Everyone calls you 'lucky.'

EXAMPLE:

You meet a new prospect interested in buying a high-ticket
product. She walks into your office and has a necklace
featuring four kid-shaped charms hanging from it. She also
mentions that she's a member of the local chamber of
commerce. You immediately identify her need for
Acceptance. Your language when you pitch your product is
tailored to this need and away from the associated fears of
social problems within her group. The other salespeople call
you 'lucky.'

EXAMPLE:

As a psychotherapist, you're introduced to a new patient
who suffers from an eating disorder. She tells you she's 'not
good' at several sports in high school and twice asks if it's
okay to grab a tissue from the box beside her. You identify

her right away as an Approval need, and provide her reassurance, and instead of giving her advice, you focus on permission. You know her disorder may be rooted in the Approval fears of being left out and unrecognized. Her therapy goes exceedingly well, and the other therapists congratulate you on having an 'easy' patient.

By no means does the Needs Map© illustrate all human needs. It merely shows us which social needs someone is expressing, and gives you a firm grip on the most effective lever of persuasive speech and communication.

SUMMARY

It's a sobering thought – all of us are drug addicts to some extent. When you identify the Needs someone is showing you in a conversation, you've identified a lot more than a location on a short list. Their entire psychology is laid open for examination, revealing their social fears that not even their families know about. Identifying needs comes at a price; you'll see people differently at first, and you'll begin to notice everyone covering up some kind of suffering. At first, it might feel like you're misreading the situation, but you aren't. In fact, everyone is suffering and insecure at times. How we cover the suffering up is one of the ways that enable you to identify Needs.

The Needs Map shows us what someone is seeking on a social level. In the next chapter, we are going even deeper; I'm going to show you what I thought I would never reveal to the public; The Decision Map. This will reveal the hidden patterns we all have that govern how we all make choices, from buying a car to deciding who to date.

LOCUS OF CONTROL

We already know how important it is to spot behavioral indicators of those we speak to. Identifying someone's locus of control will help you avoid conversational pitfalls that could cost you a loss of 'behavioral capital.'

Locus of control refers to how much people believe they, as opposed to external forces, are in control of the outcome of someone's life. People with an internal locus of control tend to view themselves as being in control of their lives. People who have an external locus of control tend to view their lives as being controlled or decided by external factors such as other people, their environment, or 'fate.'

Does someone typically attribute their successes and failures to chance, luck, and circumstances, or skill, talent, or personal behavior?

External Locus of Control:
These people tend to blame others rather than themselves for what happens in their lives. These people tend to believe they have less control over their fate. Surprisingly, these people are less likely to suffer from clinical depression.

Internal Locus of Control:
People with an internal locus of control tend to view themselves as being in charge of their own fate. They are, however, also more prone to stress and depression. Some studies even suggest that these people are more likely to enjoy success and achievement in their lives.

Locus of control can affect many aspects of our lives. People suffering from some medical conditions, for instance, are more likely to attribute these conditions to their choices or their genetics based on their locus of control. People who gamble are also more likely to be external-locus people, as internal-locus folks are less likely to take risks at a casino than their internal-focused counterparts.

In many studies, it has also been found that Republicans are far more likely to have an internal locus of control, and democrats will more often share an external locus of control.[1]

In behavioral psychology, the most widely used tool to assess a person's locus of control is called the 13-Item Forced-Choice Scale[2]. This assessment contains questions to assess locus of control, but this is still reasonably easy to assess in conversation within the first few minutes. The questions on the Forced-Choice Scale contain two-question choices that force a participant to choose one. Some examples are:

- Many of the unhappy things in people's lives are partly due to bad luck
- People's misfortunes result from the mistakes they make.

---

[1] Locus of control and political participation of college students: a comparison of unidimensional and multidimensional approaches | Gootnick, Andrew T. | University of Arizona | 1944

[2] Generalized expectancies for internal versus external control of reinforcement | Rotter, J.B. | Psychological Monographs (80), Number 609 | 1966

- One of the major reasons we have wars is that people don't take enough interest in politics.
- There will always be wars, no matter how hard people try to prevent them.
- In the long run, people get the respect they deserve in this world.
- Unfortunately, an individual's worth often passes unrecognized, no matter how hard he tries.
- Becoming a success is a matter of hard work; luck has little or nothing to do with it.
- Getting a good job depends mainly on being in the right place at the right time.
- The average citizen can have an influence on government decisions.
- This world is run by the few people in power, and there is not much the little guy can do about it.
- When I make plans, I am almost certain that I can make them work.
- It is not always wise to plan too far ahead because many things turn out to be a matter of luck anyway.
- What happens to me is my own doing.
- Sometimes I feel that I don't have enough control over the direction my life is taking.

When we hear people speak about almost anything, they will show us their locus of control. If we encounter someone with an internal locus of control and continue to talk about luck, chance, or fate, for example, we may lose them. When I prepare law firms for trials, this is a vital piece of information they need to know when they are selecting their jury. If you're wanting a jury to side with a big company who's up against a lazy person suing them for spilling hot coffee on themselves, you'll want a jury with an internal locus of control; people who believe their lives are in their own hands. Someone who thinks reading a 'Caution! Contents are HOT!' label isn't necessary for intelligent people.

If you're selecting employees in job interviews, you know that people who have an internal locus of control are more likely to be hard workers.

KNOWLEDGE CHECK

1. If someone complains about how often they get sick, what Need are they showing you? What would their social fear be in that situation? What do you think their locus of control would be?

2. If your boss is Significance and Power/Strength, how would you approach a conversation where you needed to persuade him? Would you ensure you remained dominant to remind him he's not as powerful as he thinks, or would you give him what he needs (a rush of chemicals)? What would this boss' locus of control be?

CHAPTER 10

THE DECISION MAP©

While the Needs Map lets us identify what someone needs in social interactions, the Decision Map reveals **how they make most of their decisions**. In sales, this will show you the thought process someone goes through before making a purchase. In interrogation, this will be the reason someone decides to confess. In the courtroom, a witness will decide to be honest, and a jury will be swayed by where they are on the Decision Map.

Download a high-resolution Decision Map at
www.chasehughes.com/6mxbookresources

You can identify people quickly on the Decision Map visually. Even looking around a department store, you'd be able to spot where someone is on the Decision Map. When we don't get compliance from a person, it's often that we are pitching the wrong decision style to them, as you'll see.

The Decision Map categories are interrelated, and people will most likely share two of the six categories.

The Decision Map consists of six 'decision factors' that filter how we make choices, from who we choose to sleep with to what car we buy. Let's first look at each of the pillars:

1. Deviance
2. Novelty
3. Social
4. Conformity
5. Investment
6. Necessity

Each of these pillars bleed into the one that's closest to them.

For instance, someone driven toward Deviance (a departure from accepted norms) will also consider Novelty (how new something is) when making decisions. Someone rooted mostly in Novelty will tend toward Social and Deviance. A person who is in the Social category will also tend a bit toward Novelty and Conformity, and so on.

THE DECISION MAP UNPACKED

Each of the Decision Map, much like The Human Needs Map©, will have an associated question. Imagine thinking through those questions and knowing someone is going through that thought process as you interact with them. It's truly magic, and the results, you'll soon see, are absolutely astounding.

If you're able to harness the power of the Needs Map and know what questions someone asks unconsciously, the six decision styles reveal yet another question that becomes the steering wheel of their decisions and actions.

DEVIANCE

- Question: Will this help me **stand out** or break cultural/social norms?

Deviance decision-makers will choose products, behaviors, beliefs, attitudes, friends, personal image, and decor based on whether the action will help them deviate from normally accepted standards. Their personal appearance is set to show others that they don't conform to typically accepted purchase behaviors and social norms.

NOVELTY

- Question: Is this **noticeably new**, and will others see it?

Novelty decision-makers will choose products, behaviors, beliefs, attitudes, friends, personal image, and decor based on whether the action will show that they are early adopters of new trends, technologies, and products. They will make decisions based on how 'new' the experience is and thrive on choosing behaviors that give them experiences they haven't had before.

SOCIAL

- Question: Will this make people around me show interest or **connect with me**?

Social decision-makers will choose products, behaviors, beliefs, attitudes, friends, personal image, and decor based on how the action will be viewed and interpreted by others. They are more likely to adapt to new fashion trends, hide their flaws, and display behaviors designed to impress or please the people around them. Their decisions are regulated by their estimation of how others will interpret their behavior.

CONFORMITY

- Question: Are others in **my peer group doing this**, and is it acceptable to them?

Conformity decision-makers will choose products, behaviors, beliefs, attitudes, friends, personal image, and decor based on whether the action will maintain their status in a social group. They typically are averse to radical shifts in behavior and will make decisions based on how it will appear to their close peer group. As conformity decision-makers choose their actions, they will consider the social implications first and whether or not their close peers are doing similar things.

INVESTMENT

- Question: Is this investment or behavior going to provide me with a **valuable return**?

Investment decision-makers will choose products, behaviors, beliefs, attitudes, friends, personal image, and decor based on how the action could affect them on an investment level. The return-on-investment is usually the guiding factor. They are prone to overanalyze unless they are primed to be completely receptive.

Just looking at this list, you can see how easy these people might be to identify from across a room. If you were in an airport restaurant, how fast could you look around the room and identify someone who's a Deviance decision maker? Pretty quick.

In a crowded restaurant, could you find the Conformity decision maker? Absolutely. They would have clothing that was chosen to conform to their culture. If you're looking at a higher-income Conformity person, you'd see the same khaki slacks that you see anywhere and the same sweater-vest that lots of other people in the same job tend to wear.

NECESSITY

- Question: What specifically makes this **necessary versus other options**?

Necessity decision-makers will choose products, behaviors, beliefs, attitudes, friends, personal image, and decor based on whether the action will fulfill a specific purpose. They weigh options more than others and will typically be more patient with decision making unless they are triggered by the limbic system to act.

BUYING A CELL PHONE CASE

Let's use something small and silly as an example to demonstrate how the Decision Map permeates into *every* aspect of our lives.

If you walked into an electronics store and stood in the aisle of cell phone cases with someone from each of the pillars on the Decision Map, you'd still be able to spot them, even if they were all wearing a disguise.

Our decisions, big or small, are filtered through one of the six pillars of the Decision Map:

The Deviance person will be looking for the case that really stands out. Maybe the one in the shape of an oversized cat, or one with bright colors or lights.

The Novelty person would be standing there, looking through the options, trying to find the clearest and minimal case possible. This would allow everyone they interact with to notice the brand-new iPhone they just bought—and probably got on the day it was released.

The Social person would be kneeling, looking at all the transparent phone cases that contained glitter. They're asking themselves, 'What's going to help me connect to others?' They might be reaching for the one with a sports team logo on it or one that draws attention.

The Conformity person would be looking for the case that doesn't stand out too much and matches the case that looks most like what everyone else has.

We all know a **Necessity person.** Everyone begs them to upgrade to a new phone. Their phone is riddled with cracks, and they assure you, 'It works just fine for me. I don't need a new one.' But let's assume they finally broke down and bought a new phone. They'd be there in the aisle, looking for either the cheapest case or the one that is going to last a lifetime.

An investment person would study the phone cases for just a little longer. They need a case that will protect the phone as much as possible, giving them the maximum return on investment for their precious new phone that they also chose because of its perceived return on investment.

We could run the same scenario in a bar, where the same six people would be choosing a potential mate. They would choose someone close to them on the six-pillars initially but would decide to move forward with the relationship based on the questions associated with each of the pillars.

From buying houses to cell phone cases, the Six decision styles tend to be the 'hand on the wheel' when we make choices and decisions. Spotting this is critical to understanding their behavior. Body language skills are no match for behavior profiling at this level.

Let's go through a few examples:

EXAMPLE: (Interrogation)
A suspect is escorted into the station, and you notice their arms are covered in tattoos. They also have hair that's dyed blue and a few nose rings. You identify them as Deviance and decide to remove your collared shirt and tie, opting

instead for a t-shirt or polo. In the interrogation room, you know the decision to confess is rooted in the question associated with their Decision Map location: Will this help me stand out or break cultural/social norms?

NOTE:

Interrogations are a lot like sales; sometimes they take a long time. If you were to go back to any online interrogation video that lasted over five hours before the suspect finally confessed, you'd notice a shocking trend. The interrogator doesn't have this training and is trying to relate to them and get information. Throughout the interrogation, they use random scenarios/techniques to convince them to confess. However, when you get right to the confession, the interrogator *accidentally* uses language and ideas that speak to the suspect's needs and decision style - the confession takes only minutes after that. Try it out!

EXAMPLE: (Dating)

You're on a second date with someone, and you are starting to like them. You identified them early on as Novelty - so are you. When you sit down to eat, you show them the brand-new phone that just came out, and you both make it a third date to get them one as well.

EXAMPLE: (Sales)

You have been introduced to a customer who is interested in buying a new home. As they walk into your office, you notice their hair, shoes, clothing, and everything else is all similar to everyone else in their income bracket. Later in the conversation, you hear them talk about friends on the golf course, the country club they belong to, and vacations they take with other couples. You've spotted the pillars of a Conformity-decision-style, and Social-decision-style, and already know exactly what angle to approach from when you show them the house.

NOTE:

Conformity is common in both high- and low-income areas. If you were to stand in the street of a fancy neighborhood in the morning, you'd no doubt see everyone walk outside to leave for work. They would all be wearing similar slacks, shirts, ties, and haircuts. They'd climb into their similar Lexus, Mercedes, or BMW and head off to work. All the grass is cut to the same length, and the yards all look remarkably similar. Even the Homeowner's Association enforces conformity for the 'good' of the neighborhood. In a low-income neighborhood, you'd see much of the same - similar clothing, cars, yards, and homes.

EXAMPLE:

You're a CIA Case Officer stationed in Europe. You've been tasked with recruiting an 'asset' to spy for the United States. As you make your first contact with the potential asset, you notice a waterproof case on their phone, a well-made shirt that is older but still looks great, and a wristwatch that looks as though it's been passed down for a generation or two. You identify the asset as an Investment-decision-style, and immediately know that your pitch to him must include how his actions will provide a return on his *investment*. His decisions will be filtered through the question associated with his pillar: Is this investment or behavior going to provide me with a valuable return?

Usually, people we speak to will identify themselves on the Decision Map within the first few minutes of conversation. If they don't, we have plenty of visual cues to help us identify or confirm our assessment.

The Decision Map is a powerful tool for *any* human interaction. It's something you can start using immediately! Try it online now. Go to a friend's social media page, and you'll start to see how quickly these decision-styles present themselves to you now.

SUMMARY

The Decisions Map© is something I *never* wanted to release to the public. Most people who see it might assume it's just another 'little profiling tool,' but I can assure you it has been the key ingredient in over a thousand interrogations. Now, it's the key ingredient in sales, jury trials, and even psychotherapy sessions worldwide. This tool, when paired with the Needs Map, is what really makes this entire system an 'X-Ray'. It was developed for the *Jason Bourne* folks, but anyone can now use the 6MX system.

Once you master these skills in the 6MX, you'll have the x-ray vision to see between all of the lines. But that's not enough. You will need to *listen* between the lines as well. In the next chapter, I'll show you the razor-sharp method to *hear* the same words you've always heard in a way that exposes deep-level psychology.

CHAPTER 11

SENSORY PREFERENCE IDENTIFICATION

So far, we've spent a lot of time exposing things that have been visible all along. This is no exception. We hear people speak all the time, but we didn't know the value in words hidden within their sentences.

This technique derives from a man named Walter Burke Barb, who, in the 1920s, wanted to create an understanding about how people learn differently.

Barb identified three ways we humans learn best:

1. **Visual** - watching or seeing
2. **Auditory** - hearing and listening
3. **Kinesthetic** - hands-on and doing

While these are great to identify learning modes, we can use them differently. Two therapists named Virginia Satir and Fritz Perls used these tools to identify communication styles in the early 1970s.

When we speak, we communicate using words that describe sensory experiences. All of us do this. We may speak mostly in visual, audio, or kinesthetic terms. When we speak with someone, they will quickly reveal their sensory preference through their language.

For example, if someone describes that they don't like a situation or person, you might hear it described using different sensory descriptions.

A **visual** person might say, "I just don't *see* why. Something doesn't *look* right to me."

An **auditory** person might say, "I *hear* what you're saying, but something didn't *sound* right to me."

A **kinesthetic** person might say, "I *get* that, but there's just something that doesn't *feel* right."

In my analysis of over 3,400 hours of interviews and conversations, people tended to use sensory words within the first three minutes and fifteen seconds of interactions with new people in social settings. This makes it ideal for the six-minute window this book owes its name to.

When we hear someone use sensory words, it's critical information. We should be adapting our communication to better resonate with the person. Not only is it more persuasive, but it also helps them to learn. Teachers, therapists, salespeople, and interrogators can all benefit from this invaluable technique.

Let's examine a list of sensory words:

VISUAL:

- analyze
- appear
- clarity

- conspicuous
- dream
- distinguish
- envision
- clarity
- examine
- envision
- focus
- foresee
- horizon
- idea
- illusion
- illustrate
- Imagine
- inspect
- look
- notice
- observe
- obvious
- outlook
- perception
- picture
- pinpoint
- scene
- scope
- scrutinize
- see

- show
- sight
- sketchy
- spot
- survey
- vague
- view
- vision
- watch
- witness

AUDITORY:

- announce
- articulate
- audible
- boisterous
- communicate
- converse
- discuss
- dissonant
- divulge
- earshot
- enunciate
- gossip
- hear
- hush
- listen
- loud

- mention
- noise
- proclaim
- pronounce
- remark
- report
- ring
- roar
- rumor
- say
- screech
- shrill
- shout
- silence
- sound
- speak
- speechless
- squeal
- state
- talk
- tell
- tone
- utter
- voice

KINESTHETIC:

- active
- affected

- bearable
- callous
- charge
- concrete
- emotional
- feel
- firm
- flow
- foundation
- grasp
- grip
- hanging
- hassle
- heated
- hold
- hunch
- hustle
- intuition
- lukewarm
- motion
- panicky
- pressure
- rush
- sensitive
- set
- shallow
- shift

- softly
- solid
- sore
- stir
- stress
- support
- tension
- tied
- touch
- unsettled
- whipped

These are all words we hear all the time in conversation. You'll notice a trend when you speak to people: they will tend to use the same sensory preference *all the time*.

Our job is to **identify their sensory preference and adapt our language to communicate with them**. If you're a visual person, and you're speaking with a kinesthetic person, for instance, you'll adapt to their behavior by using that person's preferred sensory words.

EXAMPLE: (Sales)

You listen in on a call one of your junior salespeople is making with someone. As you listen, the customer on the phone is using all auditory (hearing) words. You hear phrases like, 'he mentioned that,' 'let's talk about it,' and 'that other guy was a bit loud and proud.' You know right away, he's an auditory person. However, your salesperson continues to use visual words when he communicates.

You're able to provide some feedback that could change his career.

EXAMPLE: (Courtroom)

You've got a witness on the stand who's been thus far uncooperative and is having trouble remembering details about a crime they witnessed. Before you approach the witness, you glance at your legal pad and see the note you made that this person is kinesthetic. By asking more questions about temperature, clothing, and textures of objects at the crime scene, you're able to trigger more memories than the witness thought they could recall.

EXAMPLE: (Conference call)

It's 4 pm. You're stuck on a video conference call with your office staff, and the boss is continuing to ramble, reducing productivity to a halt. You'd like to wrap things up. You know the boss is an auditory person, so you politely state, "I know everyone here has *heard* all the instructions, and *listen*, I think the team got your message *loud and clear*. That was really well *said*. Does anyone have any questions the boss needs to *hear*? I know he's busy."

Sensory preference doesn't only reveal itself in spoken language. If you look online, people reveal all kinds of data from the 6MX process on their social media interactions. Before your next meeting, you can even take a look online and identify your client's sensory preference and much more.

SUMMARY

Sensory words are not only how we communicate. As you hear them, these words, are revealing the secrets to how people need to be communicated *with*. Wherever you happen to be, you'll hear sensory words every day. Let these words become more important to your brain as time passes. You'll start *hearing between the lines* in no time at all.

In the next chapter, I'm going to show you a, never-before-released, technique I developed that allows you to do even more listening between the lines. It will also show you exactly how to persuade anyone with their own thoughts.

CHAPTER 12

PRONOUN
IDENTIFICATION

The second skill you'll develop with language analysis is pronoun identification. When we speak, we tend to reveal how we think in more ways than our sensory preference. When you identify which pronouns someone uses, you can begin speaking 'their' language. I use the word *pronoun* here loosely. It's not just pronouns we're looking for, but the style of communication.

There are three categories of pronouns:

1. Self
2. Team
3. Others

The self-pronoun-users will speak mostly about themselves and use those pronouns in their speech. This doesn't make them selfish or self-absorbed. It simply means this is the way they think and communicate.

Team-pronoun-users will use words that refer to communities. Words such as we, they, us, and our will fill their language. Which of the Six Pillars would you guess these people are? What about the Needs Map?

Others-pronoun-users are less common, making up, in my estimation, around 20% of the population. These people will focus their language on people outside of their groups. Their language will focus on meeting new people, networking, and travel to novel places.

Let's look at a few examples of pronoun-users. Imagine asking a friend how they like their new job. What would each pronoun-person sound like?

SELF PRONOUNS

"**I** love it! **I've** got a corner office, **my** medical benefits are way better than **my** last company, and **I** get along with the boss really well. **I** don't think **I've** worked anywhere better in **my** life. **I've** even got **my** own parking spot there!"

TEAM PRONOUNS

"**Everyone** there is really great! **We** all have **our** own offices, thank God. The entire **team** there gets along really well, and **everyone** even has **their** own parking spots. It's so easy to communicate with **everyone** there - so much better than the other company. **They** even all go out on Thursdays for margaritas!"

OTHERS PRONOUNS

"Man, **that** company is awesome. Great **bunch** of people for sure. I get to travel a lot, and it's a lot of fun being in **new cities** all the time. **The company** even funds these **networking** dinners where we get to meet our **counterparts** in the **other company**. It's been really good so far. Lots of **good people** there. I could totally **introduce** you."

What if you asked someone you know about a vacation they recently went on?

SELF PRONOUNS

"It was really great. **I** had a wonderful time. **I** really didn't want to come back. **I** mostly spent **my** time on the beach, and **I** went to a few museums."

TEAM PRONOUNS

"**We** had a blast! My **wife and I** really didn't want to come back. **We** spent most of **our** time on the beach, and **we** went to a few museums."

OTHERS PRONOUNS

"**It** was fantastic. I **met** so many people. On this tour, I sat next to a **group** of stock advisors who are *actually* from here. At the hotel one evening, I **ran into a woman** in the hotel bar who does advanced Microsoft Excel and could really help on this project..."

EXAMPLE: (Sales)

You've watched a younger salesperson speak to a client. The client used Self pronouns the entire conversation. As your salesperson explains the benefits of the product, you hear them describing the benefits in terms of Team pronouns; discussing family, coworkers, and social circle of the client. You're able to coach them right away and change the course of their career (and life).

EXAMPLE: (Business)

Your new employee comes into your office to discuss an issue they're having; they aren't getting along with someone they've been paired with for a project. The new employee says they seem to disagree on all of the issues regarding the client-facing portion of a new system. You hear the new employee use 'Others' pronouns throughout their discussion and already know the other employee is a Self-pronoun user. After bringing them both into the room, you are able to bring their attention to this and resolve the issue, pointing out that each of them views things through a different lens.

KNOWLEDGE CHECKPOINT

Identify the pronoun type for the following short sentences:

1. "We had a wonderful time at the event! Everyone had awesome costumes!"

2. "The party was amazing. Even with masks on, I got to meet so many awesome people."

3. "I had a blast. I had a 1980s costume on, and my fake mustache fell off into my beer."

SUMMARY

Identifying pronoun usage isn't just a tool to identify **which words you need to use when speaking to someone**. This technique also gives you a window into how they view the world. When you hear which pronouns people use most, you're getting a behavioral data point that will change your future communication with that person.

When addressing a larger group, you *now* know that you will need to present information in such a way as to speak to *all three types* of pronoun users. The people in that larger audience will be a mix of all of them; Self, Team, and Others pronoun-users.

Already, you can hear more than anyone you know. Everyone you speak to reveals personality and behavioral traits through their language.

In the next chapter, I'll cover another powerful way to listen between the lines. Coming up, I'll show you a powerful method that makes language irresistibly persuasive, but *only* when you know how to listen for it.

CHAPTER 13

THE USE OF ADJECTIVES

The final linguistic tendency we need to identify is which adjectives our clients are using. Inevitably, in any conversation, we will use adjectives to describe things. If you know how to use elicitation, you can open the valve a little more, allowing more adjectives to come out.

We use adjectives to modify nouns. Someone may describe an aspect of a recent vacation as 'amazing,' while another might describe a party they went to as 'incredible.'

These are essential words. They aren't just important for us to hear in conversations, though. When we hear someone use an adjective, we need to go through a simple process in our mind:

1. Identify the context (negative or positive)
2. Keep the adjective in its list

We identify the context by merely determining whether the adjective was used to describe something the person liked or didn't like. If they were describing dealing with another company they didn't like at all and used the word 'awful,' we would put that into our mind in the negative adjective column. If they spoke of when they first met their significant other and described the evening as 'unbelievable', we would add that to this person's positive column.

In your mind, just imagine the words going into a two-column list as you speak with someone.

With pronouns, sensory preference, and adjectives, it might seem a little overwhelming at first. I recommend only learning to spot one of these at a time. Next time you hear someone speak, let your mind do its magic, placing highlights onto those words. You might bold them in your mind as you hear someone speak. The way you're going to use the adjectives is really powerful, and we'll cover that in just a moment.

Consider the following paragraph:

You asked someone what they liked about their previous job, and you receive this response.

"Well, I really enjoyed most of it. The people we worked with there were fantastic. They had an amazing system for us all to collaborate on projects, that was perfect in my opinion. Everyone loved it. The management, though, seemed to be lacking. They would come up with these horrible new ideas every week and try to get us all to implement them. I couldn't see why. It looked like they were just ignorant of our input. They would have these bright ideas every week that no one really enjoyed."

- What adjectives did you notice?
- Were you able to identify the positive and negative adjectives?
- What about this person's pronouns?
- Did you also notice the sensory words they used?

Let's look at it one more time with the important parts of the statement underlined.

"Well, I really enjoyed most of it. The <u>people we worked with</u> there were <u>fantastic</u>. <u>They</u> had an <u>amazing</u> system for <u>us all</u> to <u>collaborate</u> on projects that was <u>perfect</u>, in my opinion. <u>Everyone</u> loved it. The management, though seemed to be <u>lacking</u>. They would come up with these <u>horrible</u> new ideas every week and try to get <u>us</u> all to implement them. I couldn't <u>see</u> why. It <u>looked</u> like they were just <u>ignorant</u> of <u>our</u> input. They would have these <u>bright</u> ideas every week that <u>no one</u> really enjoyed."

You might *immediately* see this person as a **team-focused** pronoun user. You're right!

If you identified they are also a **visual communicator**, you're spot-on!

They also expressed a few descriptive words when they referred to things they liked and didn't like. In this example, let's look at the list.

Positive adjectives:

- Fantastic
- Amazing
- Perfect

Negative adjectives:

- Lacking
- Horrible
- Ignorant
- Bright (also a visual word)

Now that you're able to identify these three linguistic techniques, what are called *'linguistic harvesting'* in 6MX, you're able to do something called 'hearing between the lines'. There's a massive amount of data hidden in language that most people will never hear. **When you can identify how someone speaks in a surgical way, things change fast.**

In interrogations, I noticed a drawn-out interrogation where the suspect and the interrogator's language were mismatched. It went like this:

Pronouns: Interrogator uses *Self*-focused, suspect uses *Team*-focused pronouns

Sensory words: Interrogator uses *visual* descriptions, suspect used only *feeling* words

Adjectives: Interrogator used suspect's *negative* adjectives to try and convince them to confess

This is an issue - a big one. When the confession came around, the interrogator, in his frustration, *accidentally* changed his phrasing around to match the suspect's. Something as simple as the language alone changed the entire outcome. I couldn't believe it. In fact, I refused to believe something so seemingly insignificant could make such a drastic difference in the outcome of an interrogation.

For years, my obsession in developing interrogation techniques was to talk people into doing things (like confessing to crimes or providing intelligence against their own country) that were probably not in their best interest. I never realized these techniques were universally applicable until 2013, when I delivered a speech at a small chamber of commerce meeting in Cleveland, Texas. A salesperson asked me to provide him with all my research. A week later, the man confessed that he owned a dozen car dealerships in the area and would like to implement this into a sales system.

SUMMARY

Adjectives reveal the inner workings of the brain in front of you. Not only can you see when things are being concealed or hidden, but you can hear exactly how the brain you're dealing with works and what that brain needs in order to be influenced.

We've covered a lot, in the next chapter, I'm going to show you how compliance and influence begin to form together as you develop a behavioral profile. How does compliance work? Let's check it out...

CHAPTER 14

HOW COMPLIANCE WORKS

Compliance works in humans the same way it does in all animals; **repetition, reward, and pain**.

If someone has spent several minutes following our behavior and train of thought, the chances are that this behavior will continue. If they agreed at the beginning of a conversation to behave a certain way, they are likely to stick to it.

While this isn't a book on persuasion *per se*, I'd like to show you a technique you can use immediately to gain more compliance from people. It relies on a simple principle; **people who follow physically in a conversation will follow mentally**.

At the beginning of the conversation, you have a critical time window to get someone to begin following your behavior and movement. If you're able to establish this early, you will have set a pattern of nonverbal compliance that remains totally unconscious in the person (or group) you're speaking with.

Imagine you're just being introduced to someone; as you move to shake their hand, and they reach for yours, you take a ten-inch step to your right or left. This small movement causes the other person to make a tiny adjustment, shifting the direction their shoulders are facing. You moved, they followed, it was unconscious.

A minute later, as you're speaking with this person, you move again. This time a little greater distance. Let's imagine you step a foot or two to the right as if you were simply adjusting your position. The person you're speaking with will make a small shift in which direction they are facing. This slight movement continues the chain of unconscious nonverbal leadership that you have created.

As they begin to tell you about a hobby, or something they are interested in, they are searching your face for signs that you share a similar excitement about their topic. In these moments, when someone is discussing something they are passionate about, they are more prone to follow your behaviors. When this happens, imagine you took a small step back of maybe a foot. This 'social vacuum' that you created will be filled when the person steps slightly forward to compensate for the space you created.

This happens most often during these times because the person is telling you about something that interests *them*. They are most vulnerable to follow movement in these times.

This is an introductory look at what I call a 'compliance wedge.' In our more advanced courses and books, this continues escalating in conversations for one core reason; if we've been following small behaviors for several minutes, our brains adapt this pattern to our thoughts and ideas as well. If we are physically following someone, our brains quickly learn to do the same psychologically.

In this book, we've spent a lot of time discussing how to see what's going on inside the mind by looking at the outer body of people. However, the reverse is just as powerful. Physical movements have a dramatic effect on our perceptions and moods.

Sitting up straight, for example, makes it easier to feel confident. Slouching makes it more difficult. When our bodies are primed for something, the mind follows much easier.

In more advanced training, one key lesson I teach to interrogators, clinicians, and salespeople alike is a technique called 'agreement prep.'

None of us get excited and make big decisions while we're leaning back in a chair, exhibiting a disinterested posture. Of course, we lean in! If the body isn't displaying signs of decision-making or excitement, it's *not* time to close the sale. The rule of thumb in this technique is to never ask someone to do something big while their back is touching a chair. But how could you make someone lean in?

Getting someone to lean forward is easy. If they are leaned back or physically showing signs of disinterest, you can hand them a pen, a glass of water, or even slide a paper across the table to them in a way that forces them to lean forward in order to read it. Once their back is off the chair, guess what you'll do next?

You've got all the verbal stuff handled, and you know exactly how to speak to them, and you've noticed *every* instance of which topics and key points made their behavior relax and show interest. You know precisely how to structure every single part of the conversation. Not only will it resonate with them, but you're also going to *manufacture* the same nonverbal signals of agreement when you bring those topics back up, no matter how briefly you decide to do it. Before we get into the scenarios that illustrate the full power of the 6MX, let's talk about how to incorporate all the elements into an easy system that can fit onto a post-it note.

CHAPTER 15

THE QUADRANT

To make it easier to learn this material, this technique brings the essential behavioral techniques into a simple, easy to use format.

There are a lot of techniques in this book. At first, they might seem overwhelming. Over the course of 20 years of developing this program for intelligence work, I created something to make it easy to learn and even easier to implement.

When we learn things, they are in our conscious mind first. After repetition, they work their way into our automatic behavior. From learning how to tie your shoes to learning how to read words on a page, it was infuriatingly difficult to begin with. Over time, our brains memorized all the steps involved in each process.

This training will work in your life the same way. Here's the good news! None of the training you're about to learn will require you to carve out another piece of your day. The small things you'll be learning are things that you will apply in conversations you're already in. **You're already talking**

to humans, so it's easy to bring this practice into your life.

If you've got a piece of paper handy, draw a plus sign about the size of a post-it note. It should just look like this:

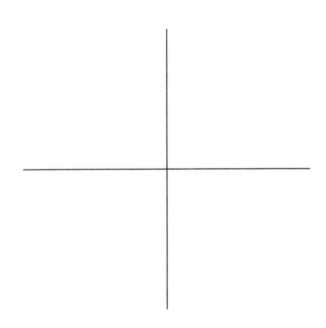

Once this is in place, add the letters as you see them in this quadrant. Each of these abbreviations indicates a piece of your 6mx training:

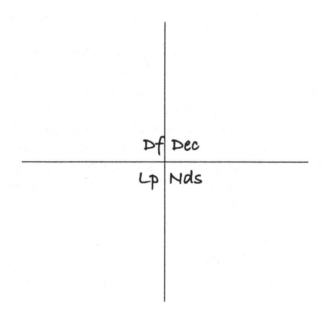

- **Df** - Digital flexion. Observing digital flexion and extension
- **Nds** - Needs - Adding the abbreviations for the identified human needs
- **Dec** – Decision Map - Identify and note the person's Decision Map style
- **Lp** - Lip movement - observing for retraction and compression of the lips

In the top-left quadrant (Df), you would only need to write an 'F' to indicate you observed *flexion* or an 'E' to indicate you observed *extension*. The flexion being a negative behavioral indicator, and the extension showing you positive emotions.

For example, if I observed flexion I would annotate this quadrant with a small 'F'. Now, my main focus is to identify the cause of this behavior; the context that may have created it. If I was speaking about our no-refund policy and observed immediate digital flexion, I would estimate this to be the cause of the behavior. Now that I am pretty sure I know what caused the behavior, I'll simply circle the 'F.' This circle means that I've successfully identified the flexion.

Depending on the scenario, you might also be able to write the topics or discussion points that cause the behavior you're seeing. For this example, let's only stick with the circles around the letters to show us that we identified the behavior and its cause.

If I saw digital extension, I would write a small 'E' and circle it if I could identify what the person responded positively to.

Inside the Needs and Decision Map quadrants, I would only need to write a small abbreviation for the person's needs. For instance, if I observed someone with Significance and Intelligence needs, I would only need to write down that's abbreviations in the quadrant. I might write 'Si' and 'In'.

The same procedure would be in place for the Decision Map. If I identify someone as Deviance, I would only write a small 'De' in the quadrant.

The bottom right quadrant being 'Lip movement', I would need to annotate when I saw lip compression or object-insertion. Both behaviors indicate negative reactions, so it would be especially important for me to identify the cause. If I observed lip compression (withheld opinions), I would write 'C'. If I observed object insertion, I would write an 'I' in the block.

If I know that the person's lips compressed the moment I mentioned their spouse, I could circle the 'C', knowing that I identified the cause. If I saw object insertion the moment I mentioned another topic, I would circle the 'I'.

You may be starting to see a trend here. When we know the cause of a behavior, we can circle it in the quadrant, letting us know we were able to identify it.

HOW THE QUADRANT MAKES YOUR TRAINING EASY

The quadrant was not meant to have only those four things within it. As you became competent in identifying Human Needs, for example, you could remove it from the quadrant altogether and add in another behavior that you will learn to spot over time.

The quadrant helps you to focus only on four or fewer behaviors at any given time. You might decide to remove the Needs from here and place in 'Shoulders', by writing an abbreviation such as 'Sh'.

In the next conversation, you would write your observations here for shoulder movements, such as shrugging behavior and dominant-shoulder-retreat movement. More on all these little abbreviations later.

USING THE QUADRANT IN CONVERSATIONS

Whether you're taking notes on a physical quadrant, or you've decided to do it all in your head, you'll need to make initial observations.

As a behavior profiler, you're going to be assessing individuals throughout your day. The initial observation (IO) is important because, as we've said before, we are looking for *change* and *movement*. The change we're typically looking for is going to be a deviation from what we initially observed.

As you begin a conversation using the quadrant, let's assume you're running a quadrant with Lips, Shoulders, Blink Rate, and Needs. As soon as the conversation begins, you would profile the lips for compression behavior and insertion behavior, you would assess the shoulders (raised or relaxed) and make an estimation of the person's blink rate (normal, fast, or slow). As the conversation progresses, you're looking for changes to these observations.

If the blink rate (which we abbreviate '*Br*') is initially normal, and you see it increase in speed, you'd draw a little upward-arrow in the *Br* quadrant, indicating an increase in blink rate. If you noticed, for example, that this happened the moment you began asking about their previous employer, you'd be able to circle the upward arrow. This would become a valuable data point that you can choose not to discuss in the future or ask more questions about later.

The quadrant follows a simple formula:

1. Make initial observations (IO)
2. Observe behavior for changes
3. Make notes of these using abbreviations or arrows
4. Circle observations where you were able to identify the contextual cause

Since this can all fit onto a small piece of paper, you can use it anywhere. But what do all these abbreviations mean? You're welcome to use whichever abbreviations you like, but let's cover how I teach our intelligence people how to use this thing.

QUADRANT ELEMENTS

Let's go over the recommended use of the quadrant. We will cover the abbreviations you can use, along with how each element is described and used in the quadrant.

Sh - Shoulder Movement

- Indicate initial observation using a dash for slightly-raised an up-arrow for raised shoulders and a down arrow for relaxed shoulders. Use the same characters to express observations of change in shoulder behavior.
- Indicate a Sh for a double-sided shoulder shrug, and Ss for single-sided shoulder shrug in conversation.
- Circle elements where you were able to identify the cause.

Df - Digital Flexion and Extension

- Indicate initial observations using 'F' for flexion and 'E' for extension.

- Indicate 'F' and 'E' later on to note observations of the movement of flexion or extension

- Circle elements where you were able to identify the cause.

Lp - Lip behaviors

- Indicate observations when observing lip compression using the letter 'c' and object-insertion using an 'i'.

- Circle instances where you were able to identify the cause of the behavior.

Ds - Dominant shoulder

- Indicate the dominant shoulder (dominant hand) with either an 'r' for right-handed or an 'l' for left-handed.

- Mark instances of any dominant-shoulder-retreat behavior with an 'r'.

- Circle instances where you were able to identify the cause of the dominant shoulder retreat movement.

Nds - Human Needs Map

Make observations on The Human Needs map and indicate them in the quadrant using an abbreviation such as:

- SI - Significance
- AP - Approval (Recognition)
- AC - Acceptance
- IN - Intelligence
- PI - Pity

- ST - Strength

It's beneficial to review the fears associated with the person's needs prior to conversations. This can also be done using online behavior profiling.

Dec - The Decision Map

Make observations on observed Six Pillars behaviors and indicators. Indicate them in the quadrant using an abbreviation such as:

- DE - Deviance
- NO - Novelty
- SO - Social
- CO - Conformity
- NE - Necessity
- IN - Investment

These should be reviewed often, as they will govern the buying behavior of your customers and decision-making strategies they will adopt in your conversation.

Br - Blink Rate

- Indicate initial observations of blink rate using a hyphen for normal, an up arrow for faster, and a down arrow for slow blink rates.
- Note changes using the same characters. If blink rate increases indicate this with an up arrow. If blink rate decreases, use a down arrow.
- Circle instances where you were able to identify the cause of behaviors you've observed.

Ss - Single-Sided Shrug
- To observe only for this behavior, which may be all you need in many cases, annotate each instance of Single-sided shrugs with an 's'.
- Circle instances where you were able to identify contextual causes.

Prn - Pronoun Usage
- Annotate with quadrant with an '*s*' for self, '*t*' for team, and an '*o*' for others.

Adj - Adjective Usage
- Annotate positive adjectives under a small column with '*p*' and the header, and '*n*' for negative adjectives as the header. These are also things you can get easily from almost anyone's online social profiles.

Sns - Sensory Preference
- Identify sensory preference words and annotate this quadrant with a '*v*' for visual, an '*a*' for audio, and a '*k*' for kinesthetic.

Bl - Breathing Location
- Identify whether someone is breathing into their chest or abdomen initially and make a note of it. Write an 'a' for abdominal breathing and a 'c' for chest breathing.
- As you notice a shift from chest to abdomen, or abdomen to chest, write the letter abbreviation of the new location. For instance, if someone is relaxed and breathing into their abdomen at the beginning of the

conversation, and they shift to breathing into their chest at the mention of a drug test, annotate this quadrant again with a 'c'.

- Circle instances where you were able to identify topics that caused the shift in behavior.

Bar - Barrier Gestures

- Make an initial note of the presence or absence of barriers.
- As barriers are either placed or removed, annotate them with 'p' for barrier-placement, and 'r' for barrier removal.

CHAPTER 16

THE BEHAVIOR COMPASS

The behavioral compass is a circular form that will enable you to fill out a behavioral profile during your training. I have some clients who use them in person and fill them out in the interrogation room in the presence of a suspect. Other clients, who wish to remain a bit more covert in conversations, will fill this compass out in their head and fill in a paper one a bit later in the conversation. There are even online models that generate random behavioral traits on a behavior compass for training.

The behavioral compass looks like this:

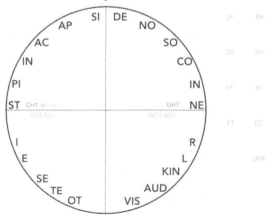

You can download one for yourself by visiting:
www.chasehughes.com/6mxbookresources

Abbreviations around the circle represent each technique you've learned in the 6MX process. Let's start by examining the top right abbreviation, 'DEC'. This area represents the Decision Map Model. At around the 12 o'clock position, you'll see the beginning of each of the abbreviations:

- **DE** - Deviance
- **NO** - Novelty
- **SO** - Social
- **CO** - Conformity
- **IN** - Investment
- **NE** - Necessity

As you identify where someone is on the Decision Map, all you need to do is simply circle the abbreviation that matches them.

Moving further down the right side of the circle, you'll see HND. This identifies *handedness*. In this instance, we are only circling R or L to indicate whether the person is right or left hand dominant. Remember, we are only identifying this to observe that dominant shoulder for retreating (backward) movement - indicating strong disagreement. Circle the appropriate abbreviation in your compass.

Below this section, you'll see SNS. This is the Sensory-Preference section. Here you'll see abbreviations for the sensory communication preferences:

- **KIN** - Kinesthetic
- **AUD** - Audio
- **VIS** - Visual

When you identify someone's sensory preference, it would be circled here. This lets you know, that in the future, you will understand how to shape your language to match the person's preferred sensory perception language.

Moving along the bottom to the next abbreviation, you'll see PRN. This is where you would circle the pronoun preference of the person you're profiling:

- **SE** - Self
- **TE** - Team
- **OT** - Others

When you hear someone's pronoun preference or you've identified it online, you would simply circle the person's preference. If you were preparing for a meeting with this person, for example, it might be helpful here to list all the pronouns you'll use in conversation to get your mind ready to speak in their specific language. This is something I still do to this day.

Just above the PRN section, you'll see LOC. This section is where you will indicate what you observed about this person's locus of control:

- **I** - Internal locus of control
- **E** - External locus of control

Knowing this, you'll know exactly how to word certain phrases in the conversation to make the person unconsciously agree with you.

The next grey appreciation you will see around the circle is NDS. This is where we profile the person on The Human Needs Map. The abbreviations follow the Needs Map:

- **SI** - Significance
- **AP** - Approval (Recognition)
- **AC** - Acceptance
- **IN** - Intelligence
- **PI** - Pity
- **ST** - Strength

If you're beginning, it helps to make a small note about the person's fears here next to the Needs you've circled before a conversation starts. This makes your conversation and discussion a lot more focused. Identifying fears not only helps you to remember them for future conversations but allows you a window into this person's personality no one else can possibly enjoy. Empathy becomes much easier to grasp.

To make it much easier to locate, I've included another copy of all the fears here in the book:

- **Significance** - abandonment, social ridicule, being ignored, feeling small
- **Approval** - dismissal, disapproval, contempt, feeling left out
- **Acceptance** - social criticism, gossip, peer mismatch
- **Intelligence** - being seen as dumb, being questioned, being 'called out'
- **Pity** - being disregarded, ignored, misunderstood, being disbelieved
- **Strength** - being "punked," disrespected, unacknowledged, challenged

On the inside of the compass, you'll see the familiar quadrant and the GHT arrows. As you identify someone's Gestural Hemispheric Tendency, you simply circle the direction they move or look in order to access positive information. If they looked to *your* right, circle the right arrow, it makes it a lot easier in conversations instead of having to continuously reverse left/right sidedness.

You can fill this quadrant with whatever behavioral indicators you'd like while you're learning. Eventually, you can add all of them into the quadrant if you'd like and develop a full behavioral profile on a single sheet of paper.

SUMMARY

Within six minutes, you should be able to fill out the entire quadrant in a conversation. Initially, it *will* take some time and may take fifteen minutes to fill this out. The next chapter will show you real-world scenarios where the Compass is applied and give you a chance to experiment with your own decisions about influence and persuasion. Let's take a look.

CHAPTER 17

HOW IT WORKS FOR INFLUENCE: CRITICAL SCENARIOS

The Behavior Compass is a tool for tracking the profile of an individual or group. Once you've collected the information to fill out a Behavior Compass, you're ready to get into serious scenarios.

The great thing about the 6MX system is that you aren't required by any means to fill the entire thing out. **If you've only got a few things on the Compass, then you're still light years ahead of anyone else who has no idea how to read people.**

In this chapter, let's walk through a few scenarios and learn how this all comes together not just on paper, but in real life.

SCENARIO 1: CLINICIAN (EMILY)

You've got a patient who has come into the office for help with an eating disorder. As you introduce yourself and spend a short time getting to know them, you're able to assemble the following Behavior Compass:

Needs: Acceptance and Pity
Potential Fears Based on Needs Assessment:
- social criticism, gossip, peer mismatch
- being disregarded, ignored, misunderstood, being disbelieved

Decision Map: Social / Conformity
GHT: Left positive
Pronouns: Team-Focused
Adjectives:
> **Positive:** amazing, cool, rewarding
> **Negative:** horrible, dark, mean, careless

Locus of Control: Internal
Sensory Preference: Visual
Handedness: Right-handed
Showed digital extension (a positive sign) when discussing *volunteer work*
Showed digital flexion when talking about a past relationship (a negative behavior)
Showed lip-compression when you mentioned medication (a negative behavior)
Showed increased blink rate when talking about self-discipline (a negative behavior)
Showed decreased blink rate when discussing journaling and drawing (a positive behavior)

You weren't able to ascertain any more data, and this is all you have to go on. For a moment, think about how *you* would approach the conversation and how you would structure your language differently for Emily. Here are a few questions to help you:

1. How would you discuss health issues with Emily?

2. Would you reference her being in charge of her life, or that she's going to have to trust that things will work out based on her locus of control?

3. You know she responds *negatively* to discussions about medication based on the Compass. How would you preface this discussion to overcome her potential objection before bringing up medication?

4. Would you speak about how *significant* and *successful* she will be as a result, or would you frame the discussion around how her *friends* and *peer group* will see her growth?

5. With Pity being her secondary need, would you be more likely to remind her to be grateful or let her know she's been through a lot and she's overcome so much already?

6. Would you convince her to seek help by framing the benefits as something that is *necessary* for her survival or something *her friends will all appreciate* her for?

7. Looking at her negative adjectives on the Compass, how would you construct a few short sentences discussing the consequences of inaction?

8. Looking at her positive adjectives, how would you describe the benefits of long-term therapy with her so that she will decide that *you* are the clinician that can help her?

9. What sensory words would you be more likely to use in all her therapy sessions in the future?

10. What sensory words would be good to describe the benefits of therapy?

11. Would you describe therapy as a **'quiet'** place to work on herself, a **'safe'** place, or a **'crystal clear'** experience that can change everything?

12. With her decrease in blink rate when discussing journaling and drawing, how could you use this information not only to get her to continue to seek help but to compare what therapy does for her to these things? If you did that, which pronouns would you focus on, and sensory words would you use?

SCENARIO 2: SALES (DAVID)

You have a new customer who'd like to arrange a recurring contract with your company. Over the phone and social media, you were able to fill out most of the Compass. When you met with David only minutes ago, you confirmed many of your assumptions and now have even more data to use to relate to him on a more human level.

Needs: Significance / Intelligence
Fears based on Needs Map:

- abandonment, social ridicule, being ignored, feeling small
- being seen as dumb, being questioned, being 'called out'

Decision Map: Novelty
GHT: Right positive
Pronouns: Self-Focused
Adjectives:

    Positive: Badass, interesting, brilliant
    Negative: nasty, ridiculous, overbearing, outdated

Locus of Control: Internal
Sensory Preference: Audio
Handedness: Right-handed
Showed digital extension (a positive sign) when discussing his new phone
Showed digital flexion when talking about paperwork (a negative behavior)
Showed lip-compression when you mentioned taxes (a negative behavior)
Showed increased blink rate when talking about product safety (a negative behavior)

Showed decreased blink rate when discussing
networking (a positive behavior)

You witnessed a **single shrug** when he told you his
company is ready to move forward (a potentially bad signal)

As you collected the information and went through
David's initial conversation, he revealed enough to almost
fully complete a single Compass.

1) How would you discuss his role in the company based
on his needs in a single sentence?

2) With his Decision Map set to Novelty, how would you
frame the service you will be providing his company to
David?

    a) The service is essential for any business to succeed.
    b) Dozens of other businesses in the area are using
    this technology.
    c) Lots of people have told us we saved the company
    when they brought us on board to assist.
    d) This is the most groundbreaking approach I've ever
    seen to xyz?

3) Which direction would you lean when you begin to
close the sale?

4) David has Self-focused speech (pronouns). What would you want to discuss most before closing him?

    a) His co-workers, and what they will think / how they will benefit.

    b) How he will benefit initially from the service.

    c) How the companies they deal with will notice the difference .

5) Given David's positive adjectives, how would you structure your close to implement them into your language?

6) Using David's negative Adjectives, how would you benefit most?

    a) Use the negative adjectives while describing the cost of business.

    b) Use the negative adjectives while discussing the local traffic.

    c) Use a few negative adjectives while describing taxes.

    d) Use his negative adjectives while describing some of the previous companies he has had issues with.

7) Which phrase is David more likely to respond positively to?

   a) Sometimes bad things happen to good people.
   b) Some people like to blame the world for their problems.

8) Which phrase would you use to discuss your deal with David during the close?

   a) Everything sounds good here. I'll talk to Sara, and she'll get it all taken care of. Sara has a good ear for details.
   b) We've got all the details firmed up. I'll touch base with Sara to get it all taken care of. Sara has a good grasp of everything.
   c) It all looks good to me. I'll see Sara, and she'll get it all taken care of. She's got an eye for that stuff.

9) David mentioned he had issues with a previous company. What would you respond with when discussing things you've heard about that other company as well?

   a) I heard a lot about them. Most people told me it was like paying taxes when you work with them. All their stuff is overused and a little out of date.
   b) I see what you mean. I get customers in here a lot saying that. There seems to be a traffic jam with all the hoops they make people jump through.
   c) Well, I'm not sure it's their fault. They're a great company; their software is just so brand new…

10) Based on your Compass data, what two subjects would you casually bring up as you built up to closing this customer? (based on positive behaviors that you observed)

    a)   Taxes and safety

    b)   Restaurants

    c)   His new phone and networking opportunities

    d)   His disdain for taxes and people who are 'victims"

It's not just a part of a conversation that changes. Every conversation changes forever. Using the compass to profile individual behavior traits is what makes the difference between the guy with a lock pick and the guy holding the key. You bought this book because results count, and you don't have room in your life for hit or miss conversations. The more you begin to incorporate this into your life, the more powerful it will become. This is only the beginning, however. I've got more in store for you…

In the next chapter, I'm going to walk you through your 6MX training step by step. I'm going to hold your hand through the process to make sure you can apply these skills in real-time and in real life.

CHAPTER 18

YOUR TRAINING PLAN

The process of becoming a behavioral operative / Behavior Pilot starts small. This will cover an outline of recommended training, exercises, and techniques to build your skill up to a surgical level.

While many read books on behavior and think to themselves that they've got things figured out, I want you to be the person that actually does it. I want you to take the vital training you've been given and translate it into a skill. Knowledge of these things does nothing. The skill does everything.

Thus far, what you've been trained in is the most powerful rapid behavior profiling system in the world. That's why the elite use this system only for their operations.

The training process for 6MX is broken down into four phases:

VISUAL

In this phase, you will grow your skills of observation. This phase specifically deals with the observation of behavior while you're speaking with someone.

AUDIO

This phase involves listening between the lines and identifying the revealing aspects of language you hear from others.

RESPONSE

This phase involves the ability to alter your language in conversations in response to information you receive from the visual and audio cues.

MENTAL

This phase of training is where you will be able to create an entire behavioral compass mentally and incorporate all of the information into unconscious responses in conversations.

THE VISUAL PHASE

This phase relies heavily on the quadrant method. Go through the visible behaviors listed in this book and begin to profile these in conversations. Limit yourself to no more than four behaviors at any given time. Some may also choose to do only one at a time.

The visual phase should last a minimum of 2 months; allowing the observation of these behaviors to become automatic.

As you become competent at automatically identifying behaviors, move them off the quadrant, and allow new ones to take their place.

You. May decide to spend an entire week identifying the blink rate. The videos you watch online, the conversations you have, and even looking across a restaurant at the blink rate will become your new 'norm'. As observing the human blink rate becomes automatic, you can add another behavior such as postural tilt. Then a week or two is spent observing nothing but blink rate and postural tilt in conversations.

As you do this, you'll notice something start to happen; you'll start to see how powerful observing each of these behaviors are on their own. Just looking for one or two behaviors gives you so much insight that you'll naturally want to continue adding new observations and behaviors to your list.

Try this with your significant other:

1. Have a movie night, but watch a reality TV show or something without actors in it.
2. Watch the episode twice.
3. Compete with each other who can spot shifts in blink rate with the volume completely turned off.
4. The second time you watch the episode, go back and turn on the volume and identify the context that caused the shift in the blink rate that you observed.
5. This trains your brain to observe the behavior and allows your brain some 'breathing room' to get that handled.

6. The second time helps your brain connect those two things, so it becomes easier the next time you observe it.

This is something you can do with your kids, a friend, or even as a 'date night'...if you're a behavior nerd like I am.

Keep in mind that you're building this skill one piece at a time. Much like building a house, you need a single brick at a time to make sure they are well-placed. Gradually add these bricks as you become confident the previous one is firmly set in place.

THE AUDIO PHASE

This phase only requires you to search for audio information. The good thing about this is that you can do this with television, podcasts, interviews, online videos, and everyday conversations.

Since you're only listening for pronouns, adjectives, and sensory preference, you can take your time with this. Listen to a podcast with the sole intention of identifying the guest's sensory preference. Listen to a conversation on TV with your eyes closed, only listening for the pronoun preferences someone has. These small steps that you can do alone will lead to increased success as you begin to layer them into real conversation.

You can utilize the audio from any conversation and hear all three of these things jumping out at you. After a few months of practice, layer the behavior profiling (visual) skills on top of the audio skills you now have. As you combine these together, you'll experience what many of my students do; it starts to feel like a superpower and can become a very healthy addiction.

THE RESPONSE PHASE

This phase is where it all begins to come together. You've mastered the art of spotting all the physical behaviors and the delicate skill of listening with the intent to hear behavior where no one else can.

In the same room as a hundred people, you'll see information flowing from people that no one else in the room is even aware of. In the response phase, you're going to focus on altering your communication to suit the other person's behaviors.

Initially, pull out a Behavior Compass, and fill it out as you watch a television show. As you fill it out, hit pause, and write out how you would word yourself differently based on the information you just gathered.

If I were selling cars, I would change my wording drastically based on the information I get. As I watch the show and fill out the compass, I'm going to pause the show, write out all the ways I might modify my language to suit the client, and verbally rehearse it. There is an exercise at this phase that is very helpful.

Consider the following questions as you develop your Behavior Compass:

1. How does my client view the world?
2. What is my client afraid of in regard to making a decision to _____?
3. How are this person's needs going to affect the decision to _____?

4. How will this person's pillar affect their decision to
   _____?

5. How will I need to diff my description of _____
   based on their needs?

6. How will I need to modify my discussion of
   _____ based on their pillar?

7. What words will I use to describe _____ based on
   their pronouns?

8. How will I relate to them using their sensory words?

9. How can I describe _____ using their adjectives?

10. Which way will I lean when I ask them to
    _____?

11. I saw _____ behavior during the mention of
    _____, how will this affect whether or not they
    will be compliant?

12. How can I respond to their digital flexion response to
    _____?

13. Based on the entire Behavior Compass, what is needed
    for this person to feel like they are the hero in their own
    story?

These are only a few questions to ask yourself. But as
you progress, this becomes automatic behavior. I can assure
you that this doesn't take as long as you might be thinking.
Small amounts of practice can sharpen these skills in no
time. And keeping logs and journals about your
development will most definitely make the process much
faster.

THE MENTAL PHASE

In this phase, you will realize your superpowers. The techniques are woven together in a perfect surgical toolkit.

To get it into the unconscious, take it one step at a time. Begin to commit changes in blink rate to memory. As you memorize the causes of blink rate shifts, your communication and language will automatically start to shift. This may initially seem as though the shift won't be automatic, but I think you'll be surprised.

Your first priority in this phase is data acquisition - remembering the behavioral profiles you observe and acting on them in real time.

Spend this time combining the other three phases and develop these skills into an unconscious process.

THE TRAINING PLAN

The following is a sample 25-week training plan for learning the 6MX process:

WEEK 1:

Spend every moment in contact with people using the four laws of behavior and seeing them through the fourth lens, 'Reasons'.

Just the daily practice of seeing people in this way will drastically change your life. This entire week, hone your skill by keeping the four laws of behavior in mind as you interact with people. People are suffering and insecure. Many times, the ways that we hide this from others becomes the mask we wear. The mask is something that forms as a means of protection in childhood. Start seeing people in this way, and everything changes.

Make a shift this week to seeing people through the eyes of the four lenses. How does seeing people through the fourth lens affect your interactions? Prove to yourself that the fourth lens is the ideal way of seeing anyone - revealing that they aren't who they seem to be initially, but a compilation of suffering, reward, and shame. Our shame governs what our mask looks like.

WEEK 2:

This week, profile the Gestural Hemispheric Tendency in everyone you meet. Notice that you can move in this direction to pitch your ideas. Watch the facial expressions in others if you move the other direction.

WEEK 3:

Spend time in every conversation profiling shutter speed and blink rate. Make notes when you can about when you saw increases and decreases in speed.

WEEK 4:

Confirmation glances show us so much. In each conversation, look to see where attention goes, and if someone glances at someone else for confirmation. Use the eyebrow flash when introducing yourself, or even at the checkout line to see who automatically returns the gesture.

WEEK 5:

The lips tell us so much. Observe the face this week and make mental notes every time you observe the mouth's two critical behaviors; lip compression, and object insertion.

It's vital to note the topic of conversation that's being mentioned as you witness the object insertion or lip compression.

WEEK 6:

The face is a superb communicator of truth. Keep an eye out any time you see facial expressions this week. Watch for the two indicators of false facial expressions, asymmetry and sudden stops of expression.

WEEK 7:

The nose and mouth are important to all of us. Watch during your interactions this week for nostril flaring, and mouth-covering (hushing) behavior. When do you observe these? Is it during a time someone is apprehensive about agreement, or it's when they become excited about something you're mentioning?

WEEK 8:

Our limbs move a lot when we speak. This week, make a mental note of where the limbs go. Do they cross across the body, cover the genitals with a 'fig leaf' or a 'single arm cross'? What was being said when you noticed these behaviors? If you see someone crossing their arms, make a mental note of whether you're seeing digital flexion or if the fingers are relaxed.

WEEK 9:

This week, look for two reliable indicators: If you're seated with someone, observe their hands. Do you see digital flexion or extension? When you see digital flexion, you know you've got work to do, and digital extension means you need to memorize the topic.

WEEK 10:

Which way are feet pointing? Since feet are such a reliable indicator of psychological intent, spend time in each conversation observing which way the feet are pointed. Determine if the person is interested or disinterested in the conversation. If you see groups of people, observe which person most people's feet are directed towards. If you're in line at the coffee shop, observe whose feet point to the cashier and whose point to the exit.

WEEK 11:

When we expose our bellies, we feel very little fear. Pay close attention to how much belly exposure you're seeing in conversations.

Secondly, how quickly can you pinpoint someone's dominant hand? See how many times you're able to identify this.

Lastly, at the beginning of every conversation, identify whether someone is breathing into their chest or abdomen. As with all of your behavior profiling skills, the key is in noticing whether this changes during the conversation. When it changes, you've obtained valuable data as long as you're able to identify the conversational context that likely caused it.

WEEK 12:

Our shoulders are strong communicators. From protecting us from large tigers a few million years ago to showing our kids we have no idea how to solve that math problem, they do a lot. This week, observe when you see double-sided shoulder shrugs and single-sided shoulder shrugs. Ignore the rest of the body and simply focus on the shoulders.

The shoulders will also show when someone is in disagreement with us. As we are able to identify which hand someone uses to write, we know that the same shoulder will 'retreat' whenever they feel a sense of strong disagreement.

Lastly, our shoulders move to show where our attention is at the beginning of any conversation. Make a small shift to build compliance-wedging and make note of whether the shoulder reorients to face you as you move.

WEEK 13:

Barriers behavior can show us a lot. I've seen it in hundreds of interrogations: the suspect picks up a cup of water from beside him, takes a sip, then places the cup between himself and the interrogator. Note any time you see increases or decreases in barrier behavior this week. Does someone place their phone in between you and them? Did you see someone reach down and button their jacket (assuming it's not freezing outside)? Were you able to pick up when someone moved an object out of the way as you interacted with them?

Note the topics of conversation when you see any barrier behavior, removal, and placement. Each of these provides you with invaluable intelligence about the situation.

WEEK 14:

We make a lot of behavioral adjustments to our bodies. During this week, make sure you're able to identify when you see hygienic gestures. When in the conversation, did that person sit up straighter? What was being said as you saw someone lick their lips? What was the detail you mentioned as you noticed someone adjust their hair?

WEEK 15:

Detecting deception is not what most people think. Most of the time, we see 'deception' behaviors when someone is simply stressed. Review the full deception section of this book and observe several videos and interactions for these indicators. Being a 'stress detector' is something that will serve you for the rest of your life.

WEEK 16:

Anytime you speak with someone this week, practice elicitation. Use the elicitation skills and challenge yourself to ask as few questions as possible. Sit down and briefly write out a few statements you can use in everyday life that can serve as your 'go to' for the time being.

As you progress through the week, note how effective the statements you are using are at getting people to open up. What might need to be tweaked or changed about the statements? Did you find yourself asking too many questions? Don't worry; it's our nature to default to questions when we need information. This takes time to develop into a practicable skill.

WEEK 17:

Revisit the elicitation chapter one more time. This week, set a goal of one piece of information you'd like to get out of everyone you speak to. For example, you may want to discover the hobbies of everyone in your office. Develop a sample elicitation statement for each of the elicitation techniques and have them handy in your phone or on a notecard.

The more you're able to use elicitation, the more information you will get. The more information you get, the more connected you become with the other person. The more they speak, the more you're able to profile them for the previous 6MX behaviors you've learned and developed skill in seeing.

WEEK 18:

The Human Needs Map can be one of the most scarily accurate tools you'll ever use. Keep the Needs written on your phone or a notecard and write down the fears on the reverse side. As you interact with people, profile their needs by listening to their words, and observing their behaviors in social settings. One trick I teach students to do is to add this data to the contact in their phones in the 'notes' section.

Write out the fears associated with nine people this week based on their Human Needs.

Secondly, go online. Check out 13 of your online friends on social media and see if you are able to determine where they are on the Needs Map based on their activity. Remember to focus your search on the information they say to others, not what they say about themselves. If you were profiling someone on LinkedIn, for example, keep a close eye on what they say when commenting on someone else's posts or offering recommendations to other people. When we speak to others, we tend to offer compliments and praise that we want to receive.

If you know them well, take a look through the associated fears. I'll bet you're able to identify an issue in the past with them that originated based on these fears.

WEEK 19:

The Human Needs Map shows us social needs, but the Six Pillars shows us how people make decisions. Whether or not someone decides to buy a car or choose a partner will be screened through the filter of the associated question on their Pillar.

Identify 12 people in person this week on the Six Pillars chart. Where do most of your close friends reside? They are most likely close to you, if not the same Pillar as you are. When you identify someone you know well, think back to when they made a decision based on their Pillar. You'll start to see a behavioral pattern that they aren't even aware of.

If you're watching an interview or television show, see how many people you can profile on the Six Pillars chart and how you would convince them to do something based on their Needs and Pillar. What would you change in your descriptions of a product? How would you convince them to try out a new restaurant? What words would you use to describe a crime to them if they were in a jury, and you needed them to convict someone?

WEEK 20:

Take along a copy of the Needs Map and Six Pillars this week. As you interact, prove to yourself you're able to profile the Needs and Pillars of anyone you speak to within a few minutes.

You can do this!

The Needs are so powerful they are literally drugs, and the pillars are how your clients will make decisions to buy from you. Get these firmly under your belt while you speak to people this week.

WEEK 21:

How many times in a few minutes can you spot sensory preference?

Take a quick look at this excerpt from an interview Emma Stone did with Interview magazine. Can you spot her sensory preference? If you look at the full interview, I'm willing to bet you can see the pattern for her sensory preference.

> "**STONE:** Like, within the hour. I remember being on the floor . . . I have never felt anything quite like that. It was so visceral. It's like someone has killed you, and you have to live through it and watch it happen . . . It was awful.
> **CROWE:** Was it a surprise?
> **STONE:** Yes. What was your first heartbreak like?
> **CROWE:** Falling off a building . . . I'm getting a stomachache just thinking about it. [Stone laughs] But creatively, do you think it's true or false that many of the artists who we know and love are often

governed by a single event that happens in their life, and that event then becomes this vivid, iconic thing they return to over and over in their work?"

From:
https://www.interviewmagazine.com/film/emma-stone

This week, listen closely for only sensory words. You'll be astonished at how reliable this one indicator is in predicting not only how people experience and remember the world, but how they like to be communicated to. The words that match their sensory preference resonate with them tenfold.

WEEK 22:

Identifying pronouns gives us an even deeper dive into how someone experiences the world. When we can spot which pronouns someone uses, we can communicate with them in a whole new way that makes more 'sense' to them.

This week, whether online or in-person, identify which pronoun preference people are. You should be able to do this a minimum of 15 times.

If you're on social media, check out the posts and comments of one of your friends. You'll learn a lot more about their view of the world than you did before.

WEEK 23:

Adjectives don't always reveal personality and behavior, but they do show us which words people like to use. When we hear positive adjectives, we can use those same words when we describe our product or service. When we hear negative adjectives, we can blend those into a discussion about something we'd like someone to avoid.

This week, identify which adjectives people use when talking about positive things and negative things. You might ask them about a vacation, then casually steer the conversation to traffic jams or their boss they don't like. You'll hear words that you now know will trigger positive and negative emotions in them.

WEEK 24:

You're well on your way. Pull out a post-it note pad and start filling out small quadrants for every interaction you have. Bring the behavioral traits you have the most trouble with into the quadrant first, and gradually rotate through them over the next several weeks until you're comfortable.

WEEK 25:

At this point, you should be able to fill out a Behavior Compass on your own.

> **The challenge**: sit with your partner or kids and watch a television show (with real people in it) and see how many items on the behavior compass you can identify.

There's even a BONUS Behavior Compass that you can use immediately. It generates a Behavior Compass for random people every time you hit 'refresh'. This training tool is a vital part of getting the skills OUT of this book and INTO your head. You can access that Random Compass Generator by going to:

https://randomcompass.herokuapp.com

Print a few of them out, and challenge yourself in meetings, watching TV, or even in person, to fill out the card.

As you progress through the year, keep a Behavior Compass handy and make sure you're continuing to sharpen these skills. They really are a superpower.

FINAL THOUGHTS

As I wrote this book, I tried to estimate the number of people who would go all the way with the training. Statistics estimate that only 2% of the people who read this book will go through with the training within its pages. This was heartbreaking to read.

My company and courses are designed to make people the most effective person in the room. I sincerely want this for you.

To encourage you to get this training done, I'm going to offer you a bonus. If you've completed the recommended training and went through the exercises, you can go to our online training center and claim 25% off the official 6MX training course.

Visit www.chasehughes.com and use the coupon code **6MXBOOKREADER** to immediately get verified and take the immersive course in 6MX online, with me!

ABOUT THE AUTHOR

Referred to as the world-leading expert by Dr. Phil, Chase Hughes retired from the US military in 2019. After a 20-year career, Chase now teaches interrogation, sales, influence, and persuasion. He developed the 6MX system for intelligence agencies, and it's now the gold standard in tradecraft.

He also works as a trial consultant, training legal teams in advanced jury selection and assisting legal teams on cases. Chase is the only trial consultant in the world who offers a whopping 300% money-back guarantee.

Chase is also the author of the #1 Bestselling book on persuasion and influence, *The Ellipsis Manual.* His in-person training events are given worldwide on how to use 'enhanced persuasion' to get behavioral outcomes.

Chase resides in Virginia with his family, where he is a beekeeping enthusiast and cyclist.

ACKNOWLEDGMENTS

I'd like to sincerely thank my editor-in-chief, **Desarae Hunter**, who has completely changed the way that I write. She dug into the trenches with me on most of my books. She can be found using the username deseraehunter online. If you're writing a book, don't do it without her! I've hired teams of editors that cost as much as a car, and they still did not come *close* to the detail, care, and uncommon level of skill she brings to bear on the craft of writing.

To **Sara**, I express my most heartfelt gratitude. She keeps the entire engine running when no one's looking. Her sleepless nights and under-appreciated contributions to my company are the reason *you* can read this book right now.

To my **kids**, who stuck with me through this, trying soooooo hard not to bother dad during 'writing time.' Thank you, guys, for hanging in there and staying so silent during all my online conference calls, where I tried to pretend like my home office wasn't in a huge open area. I am immensely proud of you.

To my cheerleader-in-chief, **my mother**. Not only does she maintain a stockpile of my books to give away to any 'worthy' passerby, but she also provided encouragement and discipline when I needed it throughout my life.

To my **dad**. I got lucky to have a man who sets an example 24 hours a day of what a man should be. I will carry that forever. His famous line throughout my childhood was, "If we can just get Chase through high school, he'll be okay."

To my **sister**, who has been the cable that tied me to 'home' wherever I was in the world. Thank you, **HP**!

Most deeply to a man I've never met who has influenced *every* aspect of my life, **Max Ehrmann**. A poem of his hung on my wall throughout my childhood, and I continue to understand it more as I mature. It still hangs on my wall to this day, reminding me that there's good in the world. I am including it here in hopes it can do the same for you.

DESIDERATA

GO PLACIDLY amid the noise and the haste, and remember what peace there may be in silence. As far as possible, without surrender, be on good terms with all persons.

Speak your truth quietly and clearly; and listen to others, even to the dull and the ignorant; they too have their story.

Avoid loud and aggressive persons; they are vexatious to the spirit. If you compare yourself with others, you may become vain or bitter, for always there will be greater and lesser persons than yourself.

Enjoy your achievements as well as your plans. Keep interested in your own career, however humble; it is a real possession in the changing fortunes of time.

Exercise caution in your business affairs, for the world is full of trickery. But let this not blind you to what virtue there is; many persons strive for high ideals, and everywhere life is full of heroism.

Be yourself. Especially do not feign affection. Neither be cynical about love; for in the face of all aridity and disenchantment, it is as perennial as the grass.

Take kindly the counsel of the years, gracefully surrendering the things of youth.

Nurture strength of spirit to shield you in sudden misfortune. But do not distress yourself with dark imaginings. Many fears are born of fatigue and loneliness.

Beyond a wholesome discipline, be gentle with yourself. You are a child of the universe no less than the trees and the stars; you have a right to be here.

And whether or not it is clear to you, no doubt the universe is unfolding as it should.

Therefore be at peace with God, whatever you conceive Him to be. And whatever your labors and aspirations, in the noisy confusion of life, keep peace in your soul. With all its sham, drudgery and broken dreams, it is still a beautiful world. Be cheerful. Strive to be happy.

By Max Ehrmann © 1927

ALSO BY CHASE HUGHES

The Ellipsis Manual - Analysis and Engineering of Human Behavior
Available on Amazon in Kindle and Paperback

Phrase Seven - A novel
Available on Amazon in Kindle and Paperback

The Collected Works of Chase Hughes
Available on Amazon Kindle

The Behavioral Training Planner
Available Exclusively on www.chasehughes.com

I worked for years to bring this system to a level that surpassed all the others. I never thought civilians would have access to it, much less a book that exposes it all. If you enjoyed this book, please consider doing me the ultimate favor of providing me an honest review on Amazon. Those things mean so very much to me, and I read every one of them.

Thank you,

WANT THE FULL CIA-LEVEL TRAINING?

Log in now to learn more about the most powerful system in the world.

Behavior Pilot™

Get your behavioral pilot's license and learn the secrets I teach our elite teams to 'pilot' human behavior. This core masterclass is only available to those who undergo a background check and interview process through my company.

www.chasehughes.com

If you enjoyed the book, please review it on Amazon!
They truly mean so much to me, and they help others discover the work I've spent a lifetime creating.

Made in the USA
Las Vegas, NV
06 January 2025

15974153R00148